EDEXCEL
GCSE MATHS
FOUNDATION

HOMEWORK BOOK

owered by MyMaths.co.uk

OXFORD
UNIVERSITY PRESS

UNIVERSITY PRESS

Great Clarendon Street, Oxford, OX2 6DP, United Kingdom

Oxford University Press is a department of the University of Oxford.
It furthers the University's objective of excellence in research,
scholarship, and education by publishing worldwide. Oxford is a
registered trade mark of Oxford University Press in the UK and in
certain other countries

British Library Cataloguing in Publication Data
Data available

978-0-19-835153-5

10 9 8 7 6 5

Paper used in the production of this book is a natural, recyclable
product made from wood grown in sustainable forests.
The manufacturing process conforms to the environmental
regulations of the country of origin.

Printed in Great Britain

Acknowledgements
Although we have made every effort to trace and contact all
copyright holders before publication this has not been possible in all
cases. If notified, the publisher will rectify any errors or omissions at
the earliest opportunity.

Links to third party websites are provided by Oxford in good faith
and for information only. Oxford disclaims any responsibility for
the materials contained in any third party website referenced in
this work.

Cover image: weter 777/Shutterstock

Contents

.1 **Place value**

1 **a** Write each of these numbers in figures.

     i   One thousand and twenty

     ii   Thirty thousand and two hundred

     iii Forty-four thousand and forty-four

     iv Three million and ten

  b Write each of these numbers in words.

     i   2300   **ii** 34 500   **iii**   102 000

     iv 255 900   **v** 999 000   **vi** 2 345 000

2 Write the number each of the arrows is pointing to.

a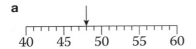
        b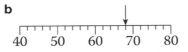

c
        d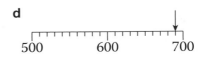

3 Put these lists of numbers in order, from lowest to highest.

  a $-4, 9, 0, -6, 12, -15$ **b** $-1, 1, 5, -9, 3, 10$

  c $12, 3, -2, 3, 0, -4$ **d** $-5, 10, -35, 13, 3, 20$

  e $0, -10, 9, 3, -5, -20$ **f** $-100, 30, 0, -29, 39, 12$

4 Calculate

  a 14×10 **b** $4500 \div 100$ **c** 2.6×100

  d 0.34×1000 **e** $156.7 \div 10$ **f** 4.568×10

  g $356 \div 10$ **h** $56\,000 \div 100$ **i** 0.54×1000

5 Calculate

  a $4 - 5$ **b** $-3 + 4$ **c** $-4 + -5$ **d** $15 - 18$

  e $14 - -4$ **f** $-4 - -3$ **g** $-3 + 15$ **h** $-10 - 3$

  i $14 + -14$ **j** $-8 - -3$ **k** $-7 + -4 + 6$ **l** $6 + -6 - 5$

6 Place the correct symbol < or > between the numbers in each pair.

  a 32   20   **b** 9.3   9.9   **c** 4.03   4.006 **d** -3 -12

1.2 Rounding

1 Round these numbers to the nearest ten.

   a 56   **b** 67   **c** 184   **d** 365

   e 436   **f** 4192   **g** 97   **h** 32.13

2 Round these numbers to the nearest hundred.

   a 453   **b** 192   **c** 76   **d** 983

   e 3458   **f** 934.54   **g** 9875   **h** 17494

3 Round these numbers to the nearest thousand.

   a 4556   **b** 9432   **c** 35467   **d** 87567

   e 294578   **f** 99483   **g** 99786   **h** 675895

4 Round these numbers to the nearest whole number.

   a 7.9   **b** 8.4   **c** 15.6   **d** 17.82

   e 36.49   **f** 36.5   **g** 105.25   **h** 496.739

5 Round these numbers to the accuracy given.

   a 46.456 (1 dp)   **b** 67.945 (2 dp)   **c** 356.4589 (3 dp)

   d 13.96 (1 dp)   **e** 34.5683 (2 dp)   **f** 13.998 (2 dp)

   g 0.6400 (3 dp)   **h** 12.705 (2 dp)   **i** 6.3575 (3 dp)

6 Round these numbers to the accuracy given.

   a 3495 (2 sf)   **b** 34.89 (1 dp)   **c** 1234 (3 sf)

   d 0.9847 (2 dp)   **e** 19.83455 (3 dp)   **f** 3298000 (1 sf)

   g 3.998 (2 sf)   **h** 12986 (2 sf)   **i** 12.0001 (3 dp)

   j 0.639 (1 sf)   **k** 1.639 (2 dp)   **l** 1.639 (2 sf)

7 Round these numbers to

   i nearest 100   **ii** 3 sf   **iii** 2 dp

   a 586.273   **b** 349.689   **c** 499.205

.3 Adding and subtracting

1 Use a mental method for each of these calculations.

    a $430 + 170$ **b** $48 + 924$ **c** $13.5 + 1.7$

    d $14.1 - 3.6$ **e** $689 - 194$ **f** $16.6 - 4.9 + 3.4$

2 Use a written method to work out these calculations.

    a $345 + 134$ **b** $734 + 154$ **c** $456 + 345$

    d $538 + 122$ **e** $672 + 245$ **f** $938 + 267$

    g $498 + 356$ **h** $932 + 834$ **i** $1234 + 546$

    j $5643 + 347$ **k** $8567 + 456$ **l** $9875 + 1896$

3 Use a written method to work out these calculations.

    a $456 - 234$ **b** $857 - 345$ **c** $984 - 232$

    d $867 - 123$ **e** $345 - 126$ **f** $567 - 329$

    g $459 - 282$ **h** $1893 - 924$ **i** $345 - 286$

    j $3458 - 535$ **k** $8947 - 5958$ **l** $4587 - 3589$

4 Use a written method to work out these calculations.

    a $54.6 + 74.3$ **b** $12.65 + 7.32$ **c** $18.34 + 8.45$

    d $16.7 - 3.6$ **e** $13.95 - 2.24$ **f** $9.78 - 3.47$

    g $143.4 + 5.8$ **h** $74.68 + 54.9$ **i** $3.667 + 6.418$

    j $98.46 - 49.54$ **k** $69.735 - 14.856$ **l** $35.67 - 29.7$

5 Use a mental or written method to work out each of the problems.

    a Karen sells fish. On Monday she sells 81.4 kg and on Tuesday she sells 66.7 kg. How much fish has Karen sold altogether?

    b A bucket full of sand weighs 19.5 kg. The bucket weighs 1.65 kg. How much does the sand weigh?

    c James is saving his money in his money box. In July he has £64.36. In August he has £56.95. How much money did James spend in August?

    d Paula is training to run a marathon. During 4 days of training she runs the following distances: 18.5 miles, 21.95 miles, 11.3 miles and 26.27 miles. Work out the total distance she runs during the 4 days.

1 Use an appropriate mental method to match the calculations with the answers. Work from left to right on each row.
What do the letters representing the answers spell?

55×8, 5×25, $88 \div 2$, 6×16, 5×32,

$96 \div 3$, 3×124, 12×10, $105 \div 5$

S = 96   E = 120   O = 44   L = 372   S = 125

E = 32   I = 440   S = 21   C = 160

2 Use an appropriate method to calculate these. Write each method you have used.

a 34×100 **b** 28×4 **c** 19×6

d $214 \div 4$ **e** $624 \div 8$ **f** 12.6×21

g 54.8×20 **h** $336 \div 6$ **i** 26.5×5

j 3.45×2.5 **k** 34×2.8 **l** 15×0.3

3 Use an appropriate method to work out each of these problems.

a $15 \times 46 = 690$. What is 15×4.6?

b 1 litre of petrol costs 129.4p. How much do 43 litres of petrol cost?

c Sonia buys 32 chocolate bars that cost £9.28. How much does each bar cost?

d Lawson drinks 2.75 litres of water every day. How much water does he drink in 2 weeks?

4 Use a written method to work out these correct to 2 decimal places.

a 25.32×9.86 **b** 1.66×5.9 **c** 64.28×4.23

d $36.24 \div 7$ **e** $5.643 \div 3.5$ **f** $1314 \div 6.22$

5 Work out each of these.

a $3 + 4 \times 5$ **b** $5 + 2 \times 6 + 3$ **c** $4 + 2 \times (3 + 5)$

d $4^2 - 16 \div 2$ **e** $18 \div 3 - 2 \times 2$ **f** $(5 + 10) \div 3$

g $\dfrac{6 + 4 \times 3}{3}$ **h** $\dfrac{4 \times 5 + 2}{11}$ **i** $\dfrac{27}{2^2 + 5}$

Q 1167, 1393, 1916, 1917   **SEARCH**

1 Write each of these numbers in words.

    a 5700   **b** 14 800   **c** 455 000

    d 200 005   **e** 800 800   **f** 8 648 000

2 Write these sets of numbers in ascending order.

    a 0.04, 0.14, 0.004, 4, 1.4

    b 3.92, 9.32, 3.29, 32.9, 0.329

3 Round these numbers to

    i 1 decimal place   **ii** 2 decimal places

    a 6.309   **b** 5.990   **c** 24.868

4 Round these numbers to 2 significant figures.

    a 0.549   **b** 0.455   **c** 0.0877

    d 0.002 568   **e** 5.155   **f** 0.000 009 459

5 Calculate

    a $6 + -3$ **b** -10×-6

    c $-3 \div 100$ **d** $28 - -9$

    e -3×-8 **f** 0.7×-100

    g $51 \div -3$ **h** $-3 + -12$

6 Use a written method to work out these calculations.

    a $45.9 + 18.3$ **b** $32.56 - 18.37$ **c** $82.5 + 9.36$

    d $12.9 - 4.38$ **e** $2.08 + 0.589$ **f** $8.03 - 0.214$

7 Use a written method to work out these calculations.

    a 41.2×5 **b** $22.75 \div 7$ **c** 15.6×0.4

    d $44.8 \div 0.8$ **e** 12.8×9.7 **f** $5.904 \div 0.18$

8 Work out each of these.

    a $6 - 2 \times 3$ **b** $4 + 2 \times 3 + 8$ **c** $(8 + 6) \times 3 - 7$

    d $64 \div 4(5^2 - 23)$ **e** $\dfrac{36}{2^3 + 1}$ **f** $(2 + 6) \times 3^2$

2.1 Terms and expressions

1   There are 9 cakes in a packet.
How many cakes are there in

   a   5 packets   **b**   8 packets   **c** x packets   **d** n packets?

2   Chocolicious makes boxes of chocolates in two sizes.
There are a chocolates in a small box.
There are b chocolates in a large box.
Write an expression for the total number of chocolates in

   a   one small box

   b   two large boxes

   c   two small boxes and three large boxes

   d   four small boxes and six large boxes.

3   Write algebraic expressions for these descriptions.

   a x add 9   **b** d subtract 10   **c** y subtracted from 8

   d   6 times x **e**   double p **f** m multiplied by 7

   g y divided by 4   **h**   one third of x **i** p divided by 3

4   Work out the value of these expressions.

   a $3a$ when $a = 4$

   b $5d$ when $d = 6$

   c $2a + b$ when $a = 4$ and $b = 3$

   d $3m + n$ when $m = 2$ and $n = 4$

   e $2x - 3y$ when $x = 5$ and $y = 2$

   f $2p + 2q - r$ when $p = 4$, $q = 6$ and $r = 5$

   g y^2 when $y = 3$

   h $x^2 + y$ when $x = 4$ and $y = 2$

5   Calculate the value of each expression when $a = 3$, $b = 4$ and $c = -2$.

   a $a + b$ **b** $3a + c$ **c** $a + b + c$

   d $3c + a$ **e** $\dfrac{2a + b}{5}$ **f** $\dfrac{2b + 2c}{4}$

   g $a \times b$ **h** $a \times b \times c$ **i** $a - b + 2c$

   j $\dfrac{3ab}{4}$ **k** $a^2 + 2a + b$ **l** $b^2 + c$

Q 1158, 1186, 1187   **SEARCH**

2.2 Simplifying expressions

1 Simplify these expressions.

a $m + m + m + m$

b $a + a + a + a + a + a + a$

c $b + b + 3b + b + b$

d $2p + p + 3p + p - p - 3p - p$

e $r + r + r + r - r - 2r$

f $a + a + a + a + b + b + b - 2a$

2 Simplify these expressions.

a $3 \times n$

b $n \times n$

c $e \div 9$

d $4n \div 3$

e $4 \times a \times b$

f $r \times s \times t$

g $2 \times a \times b$

h $p \div q$

3 Simplify each of these expressions.

a $4k - 2k$

b $4y - y$

c $5x + 2x - 3x$

d $12j - 5j + 2j$

e $k - k$

f $6p - 5p + 4p + 3p$

4 Simplify these expressions.

a $x + x$

b $a^2 + a^2 + a^2 + a^2$

c $b \times b$

d $2 \times e \times f$

e $3 \times 5 \times a \times a$

5 Simplify by collecting like terms.

a $3a + 5b + 2a + 6b$

b $8d + 4c + d - c$

c $10r + 5s + 3r - 2s$

d $11p - 3q + 4p - 2q$

e $9g + 5h - g - h$

f $5t + 3s + 6t - 3s$

g $9w + 4f - 5w - f - 4w$

h $11m + 5s - 11m - 5s$

6 Simplify these expressions.

a $4x + y + 3x$

b $8x - y + 2y$

c $x - 3y + 2x$

d $x - 4y + 6z - 5x - 6x + y$

e $6x + y - 4x - y + 2x$

f $9x - 4y + 2x - 6y$

g $x + y - x - y$

h $9x + 6y - z - 4y + 2z$

2.3 Indices

1 Write these expressions using index notation.

    a $y \times y \times y \times y$ **b** $2 \times r \times r \times r \times s \times s$

    c $3 \times b \times b \times a \times a \times a$ **d** $a^2 \times a^4$

    e $r^3 \times 3r^2$ **f** $b^3 \times b^2 \times b$

    g $3r^2 \times 2r^3$ **h** $5p^3 \times 3q^2$

    i $4b \times 2b^3$ **j** $\dfrac{p^3}{p^2}$

    k $\dfrac{z^5}{z^2}$ **l** $\dfrac{g^3}{g}$

2 Simplify these expressions.

    a $\dfrac{a^3 \times a^3}{a^2}$ **b** $\dfrac{q^5 \times q^2}{q^4}$ **c** $\dfrac{k \times k^3}{k^2}$

    d $\dfrac{t \times t^3 \times t^2}{t^4}$ **e** $\dfrac{u^4 \times u^3 \times u^2}{u}$ **f** $\dfrac{s \times s^2 \times s^2}{s^3 \times s}$

    g $\dfrac{p \times p \times p^3}{p^2}$ **h** $\dfrac{r^5 \times r \times r^2}{r^3}$ **i** $\dfrac{v^5 \times v^3 \times v}{v^4}$

3 Simplify these expressions.

    a $4p^2 \times 3$ **b** $4r^2 \times 2s^3$

    c $4m^3 \times 2m$ **d** $\dfrac{y^2 \times y^3 \times y^4}{y \times y^5}$

4 Simplify these expressions.

    a $a^2 \times a^5$ **b** $\dfrac{x^3}{x^7}$ **c** $\dfrac{y^6}{y^3 \times y}$

5 Simplify these expressions, where possible.

    a $4x \times 3y$ **b** $2p \times 4p$

    c $a \times a \times 3a$ **d** $5ba + 3ab + bc$

    e $3m - n + 4n + 2m$ **f** $x^2 + 3x^3 - 2x^2$

    g $\dfrac{6gk}{3k^2}$ **h** $\dfrac{8y^4}{y^3}$

Expanding and factorising 1

1 Expand the brackets in these expressions and simplify where necessary.

a $3(x + 5)$ **b** $4(x - 4)$

c $x(x + 4)$ **d** $2(2x + 5)$

e $-3(x + 3)$ **f** $-2x(x + 4)$

g $3(x + 4) + 4(x - 4)$ **h** $3(x - 4) + 6(x - 2)$

i $5(x - 2) + 7(x + 3)$

2 Expand and simplify these expressions.

a $3(x + 4)$ **b** $4x(x + 5)$

c $2x(x - 5)$ **d** $x^2(x + 4x)$

3 Expand and simplify these expressions.

a $3(2x + 3) + 5(2x + 4)$ **b** $4(2x + 4) + 2(4x + 3)$

c $4(3x + 2) + 3(2x + 3)$ **d** $2(3x + 5) + 4(4x + 5)$

e $2(5x + 4) + 4(7x + 3)$ **f** $2(3x + 3) + 5(x + 3)$

g $4(2x + 3) + 4(x - 2)$ **h** $3(2x + 3) + 6(3x + 3)$

i $5(x + 3) + 5(4x - 3)$ **j** $7(2x - 4) + 3(3x + 1)$

4 Factorise these expressions.

a $2x + 14$ **b** $5x + 20$

c $4x + 8$ **d** $3x - 9$

e $6x + 8$ **f** $12x + 4$

g $10 - 5x$ **h** $22x + 6$

i $20 + 4x$ **j** $16x - 10$

5 Factorise these expressions.

a $x^2 + x$ **b** $3x + x^2$

c $3x^2 + 3$ **d** $4x^2 + 2x$

e $3x^3 - 6x$ **f** $5x^4 + x^3$

g $x^2 - 4x$ **h** $4x - 12x^2$

i $5x^2 + 25x$ **j** $10x^2 - 2x$

1 There are p cereal bars in a box.

    a Write the number of cereal bars in
       i 2 boxes   **ii** 10 boxes   **iii** y boxes

    b Ranee opens a box and eats two cereal bars. Write an expression for the number of cereal bars left in the box.

2 Work out the value of each expression.

    a $4d + 4f$ when $d = 5$ and $f = 2$

    b $2m + 6n$ when $m = 2$ and $n = 3$

    c $3p - 5q$ when $p = 10$ and $q = 3$

    d $3e - 2d + f$ when $e = 1$, $d = 2$ and $f = 9$

    e $2b + 3e$ when $b = -4$ and $e = 3$

    f $4t - 5r - s$ when $t = 5$, $r = 2$ and $s = -4$

3 When n is 6, work out the value of $2(n + 3)$.

4 Simplify these expressions.

    a $3a + b + 3a + 2b$ **b** $5d + 4e - 2d + e + d$

    c $4f + 5g + 6f - 7g + f$ **d** $4h - i + 3h - 5i + h$

    e $3j + 5k + k - 5k - k$ **f** $6l + 4m - 5l - 4m - l + m$

5 Expand and simplify these expressions.

    a $3(x + 3) + 3(x - 2)$ **b** $4(3x + 4) + 3(x - 3)$

    c $5(2x + 4) - 4(x + 3)$ **d** $4(3x - 2) - 4(x + 3)$

    e $3(3x + 4) - 4(2x - 3)$ **f** $5(x + 3) - 4(2x - 2)$

    g $5(2x - 3) - 4(3x - 2)$ **h** $2(2x + 4) + 3(2x - 4)$

    i $4(x + 4) - 4(x - 4)$ **j** $2(2x - 1) - 4(x - 1)$

6 **a** Factorise $x^2 - 4x$.

    b Simplify $d^5 \div d^3$.

    c Expand and simplify

      i $5(x + 4) + 4(x - 6)$ **ii** $3x^2(x + 4) + 3(x^3 - 2)$.

7 **a** Expand $x(4x^2 + 3)$.

    b Simplify $3x^3y \times 4x^2y^2$.

    c Factorise $5x^3 + 12x$.

Angles and lines

1 a Draw a rectangle and label the perpendicular sides with └ .

b Draw a parallelogram and label the parallel sides with → and ↠.

2 Calculate the size of the angles marked by letters in each diagram.

a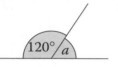

b

c

d

e

f

3 Find the value of the angles marked by letters.

a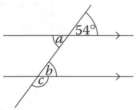

b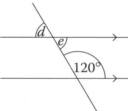

4 This map shows the position of several cities and towns.

× Stoke-on-Trent

× Nottingham

N

× Leicester

× Birmingham

× Coventry

× Northampton

Measure and write down the bearing of

a Coventry from Birmingham

b Northampton from Coventry

c Stoke-on-Trent from Nottingham

d Leicester from Northampton.

3.2 Triangles and quadrilaterals

1 Calculate the size of the angles marked by letters.

a    **b**   **c**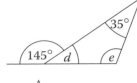

d 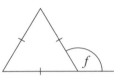   **e**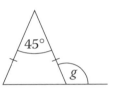

2 a Copy this coordinate grid.
Plot these coordinates
(4, 2), (−2, 3), (−4, 2).

b Find the fourth coordinate
to make a kite.

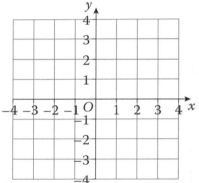

3 Work out the size of the angles marked by letters.
Give a reason for each answer.

a 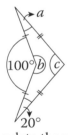   **b** 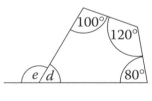   **c**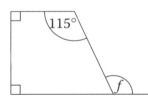

4 Calculate the value of *x* for each quadrilateral.

a 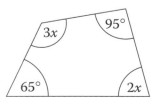   **b**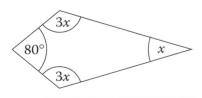

       Q 1082, 1102, 1130, 1141   **SEARCH**

3.3 Congruence and similarity

1 a Find all the pairs of shapes that are congruent.
   b Name each shape.

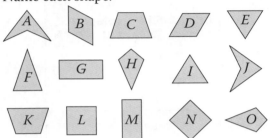

2 Which of these pairs of triangles are congruent? Give
   reasons for your answer.

a 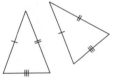   **b** 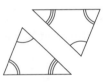   **c**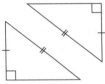

d 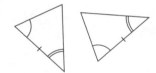   **e**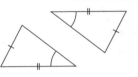

3 Calculate the value of the length marked by a letter.

a 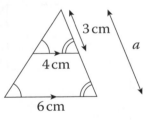   **b**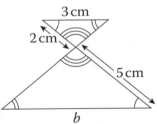

4 In this diagram

   a Show that angle *DCE* = angle *ACB*.
   b Show that angle *BAC* = angle *DEC*.
   c Prove that triangle *ABC* is congruent
       to triangle *CDE*.

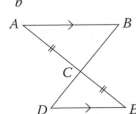

Polygon angles

1 **a** Copy and complete the table.

Shape		Number of lines of symmetry	Order of rotational symmetry
Rectangle			
Regular octagon			
Parallelogram			
Regular pentagon			
Rhombus			

b Extend the table by adding in some other well known two-dimensional shapes.

2 **a** Copy and complete this table.

Shape name and number of sides	Shape	Number of triangles	Sum of interior angles
Triangle 3 sides		1	$1 \times 180° = 180°$
Q _____ 4 sides		2	$2 \times 180° = 360°$
P _____ 5 sides			$\square \times 180° = \square$
H _____ 6 sides			$\square \times 180° = \square$

b Extend the table up to an eight-sided shape.

3 Calculate the size of the unknown angles in these polygons.

a

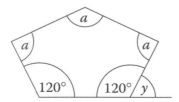

b

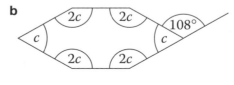

Q 1100, 1320   **SEARCH**

3

1 **a** Work out the size of the missing angle, x.

   b Give a reason for your answer.

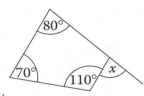

2 Calculate the size of the angles marked by letters in each diagram.

a

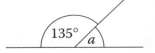

b

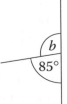

c

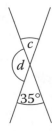

d

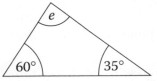

e

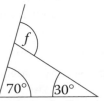

f

3 Calculate the size of the missing angles in each diagram.

a

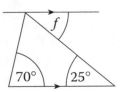

b

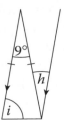

4 Find the pair of congruent triangles.

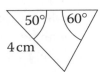

5 A regular polygon has 20 sides.

   a Calculate the size of an exterior angle.

   b Calculate the size of an interior angle.

4.1 Sampling

1 Jessica uses a data collection sheet for a survey to find her class' favourite type of film.

She limits the choice to Romance (R), Comedy (C), Adventure (A), Drama (D), Horror (H) or Other (O).

H A C C C O A O R R D H O C D
A O H R C A O C O R H D A R C

a Construct a data collection sheet to show this data.

b State the class' favourite type of film.

2 a Decide whether each of these methods is random.

i Selecting the first student from a register.

ii Putting everyone's name into a hat and picking one.

iii Selecting your closest friend.

iv Number all students from 1 – 99 and roll a 0 – 9 dice twice to generate a 2-digit number.

b Describe a method of random sampling that is different to any method described in part **a**.

3 For each of these surveys, suggest reasons why the chosen sample may be biased.

a To find out the most popular holiday destination by asking people as they leave a travel agent's office.

b To find out the most popular brand of washing powder by asking people as they go into a supermarket at 11 a.m. on a Tuesday.

c To find out how people travel to school by telephoning all the households on one page of the telephone directory on a Wednesday.

4 A machine produces bottles with screw caps. Every 20th bottle is produced with a cap that does not seal the bottle. A worker notices one faulty cap and decides to take a systematic sample of bottles in order to assess the scale of the problem. Explain the effect of sampling

a every 20th bottle, beginning at bottle number 20

b every 5th bottle, beginning at bottle number 5

c every 5th bottle, beginning at bottle number 3.

> Hint: Work out the proportion of faulty bottles in the sample taken and decide on the most likely conclusion of the factory worker.

 Q 1212, 1248, 1249 **SEARCH**

Organising data

1 Andrew is a fisherman and wants to find out which fish people prefer.
He asks 30 people to choose their favourite from cod (C), mackerel (M),
plaice (P) and sole (S).

The results were

C	C	M	P	P	S	C	C	P	P
C	M	C	P	M	C	C	P	C	C
C	C	M	P	M	C	P	P	S	S

a Copy and complete this
frequency table to
show the results.

Type of fish	Frequency
Cod	

b State the favourite type of fish.

2 These results show how many TVs are owned by students' families.

Number of TVs	0	1	2	3	4	5
Number of students	1	7	12	13	5	1

a How many students were included in the survey?

b Calculate the total number of TVs owned by all of the students.

3 A group of 36 students can choose either French or Spanish as an option.
Copy and complete the two-way table.

	French	Spanish	Total
Boys	8		
Girls		11	
Total	16		

4 The resting pulse rates, in beats per minute (bpm), of
30 athletes are given.

56	74	63	72	83	49	58	59	79	48	73	77	89	57	64
61	69	75	76	81	70	72	84	52	44	57	74	75	81	77

a Copy and complete the
stem-and-leaf diagram.

b Reorder the data to give an
ordered stem-and-leaf diagram.

```
4 | 9  8  4
5 |
6 |
7 |
8 |
```
Key: 4 | 9 means 49 bpm

Representing data 1

1 The pictogram shows the number of different colour cars that passed a school during one day.

Red	☐| ☐| ☐| ☐|
Silver	☐| ☐| ☐| ☐| ☐|
Blue	☐| ☐|
Black	
Other	

Key: ☐| represents 4 cars

a Copy and complete the diagram to show 8 black cars and 14 other cars

b Which colour car was the most popular and how many of this colour car were seen?

c How many cars were seen in total?

2 60 people were asked to name their favourite colour.

The results are shown in the table.

Draw a bar chart to represent this information.

Colour	Frequency
Red	15
Blue	12
Green	18
Purple	5
Black	2
Other	8

3 The favourite types of film for boys and girls are shown in the bar chart.

a Action was the favourite type of film for how many
  i boys   **ii** girls?

b What type of film did more girls like than boys?

c Calculate the total number of boys and girls in the survey.

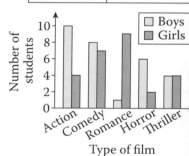

4 Charlotte did an investigation into her friends' favourite sports and recorded the results in this bar chart.

Write down two things that are wrong with Charlotte's bar chart.

 Q 1193, 1205 **SEARCH**

.4 Representing data 2

1 James received £90 for his birthday and he decided to spend it as shown in the table.

Draw a pie chart to show this information.

Computer game	£36
Sweets	£2
Trainers	£29
DVD	£17
T-shirt	£6

2 The pie chart shows the favourite sports for 90 students.

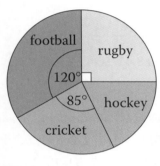

Not drawn accurately

Find

a the angle for rugby

b the angle for hockey

c the angle that represents 1 student

d the number of students who like

    i rugby   **ii** hockey   **iii** cricket   **iv** football.

3 In a city, 1800 cars were stolen in a year. The table below shows the times of the day when they were stolen.

Time	Number of cars
Midnight to 6 a.m.	700
6 a.m. to midday	80
Midday to 6 p.m.	280
6 p.m. to midnight	470
Time unknown	270

Draw a pie chart to show this information.

Averages and spread 1

1 Calculate the mean for each set of numbers.

    a 4, 5, 5, 6   **b** 12, 9, 10, 8, 11

    c 105, 102, 95, 98, 101, 99   **d** 6, 9, 8, 13, 0

    e 1, 4, 4, 4, 4, 5, 6   **f** 0, 0, 3, 2, 5, 12, 4, 4, 6

    g 3, 4, 5, 5, 4, 2, 6, 7

2 Work out the median for each set of numbers.

    a 7, 8, 12, 4, 3   **b** 1, 5, 8, 7, 4, 1, 7, 4, 3

    c 0.45, 0.38, 0.12, 0.50, 0.75   **d** 32, 35, 33, 26, 37, 54, 23, 26

    e 5.4, 4.6, 5.1, 4.5, 4.9, 5.3   **f** £3.45, £8.45, £0.45, £9.03, £4.59, £3.9

    g $1\frac{1}{2}$, 3, $4\frac{1}{2}$, 5, $3\frac{1}{4}$, 4, 5, 3, $4\frac{3}{4}$, 5

3 Calculate the range and mode of each of these sets of numbers.

    a 7, 8, 12, 8, 3   **b** 1, 5, 8, 4, 4, 1, 7, 4, 3

    c 0.45, 0.75, 0.12, 0.50, 0.75   **d** 32, 35, 33, 26, 37, 54, 23, 26

    e 5.4, 4.5, 5.1, 4.5, 4.9, 5.3   **f** £3.45, £0.45, £0.45, £9.03, £4.59, £3.9

    g $1\frac{1}{2}$, 3, $4\frac{1}{2}$, 5, $3\frac{1}{4}$, 4, 5, 3, $4\frac{3}{4}$, 5

4 This is the data Priya collected on the amount of pocket money, in pounds, that she received over 15 weeks.

    10 8 10 6 10 12 5 8 9 50 14 15 5 10 8

    a Find, for this set of numbers

        i the mean   **ii** the mode

        iii the median   **iv** the range.

    b What effect did the £50 have on each of your answers in part **a**?

5 In an English test the boys' mean percentage score was 56% and range was 12%. The girls' mean score was 62% and range was 23%. What can you say about the performance of boys compared to girls?

Q 1192, 1202, 1254   **SEARCH**

1 **a** Describe what is meant by a **random sample**.

   b Explain why choosing 15 of your friends to complete a
     survey is not a random sample.

2 A fruit seller sells 180 pieces of fruit in a day, as shown in the pie chart.

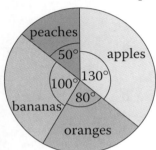

   a Calculate the angle that represents one piece of fruit.

   b Find the number sold of

   i bananas   **ii** peaches.

   c State the modal fruit sold.

3 Calculate the **i** mode **ii** median **iii** mean of each set of numbers.

   a 1, 4, 4, 4, 4, 5, 6

   b 0, 0, 3, 2, 5, 12, 4, 4, 6

   c 3, 4, 5, 5, 4, 2, 6, 7

   d 15, 16, 12, 13, 16, 12

   e 2.4, 1.5, 2.5, 1.7, 2.8, 2.3, 1.5, 1.3

4 Mrs Edwards gives her class a Maths test.

   Here are the test marks for the girls.

   7, 5, 8, 5, 2, 8, 7, 4, 7, 10, 3, 7, 4, 3, 6

   a Work out the median.   **b** Work out the range.

   The median mark for the boys was 7 and the range of the marks of the
   boys was 4.

   c By comparing the results explain whether the boys
     or girls did better in the test.

5.1 Decimals and fractions

1 Copy this rectangle 5 times. Shade each rectangle to show these fractions.

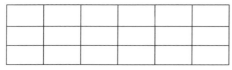

   a $\dfrac{1}{2}$ **b** $\dfrac{3}{4}$ **c** $\dfrac{1}{3}$ **d** $\dfrac{4}{9}$ **e** $\dfrac{5}{6}$

2 Write each fraction in its simplest form.

   a $\dfrac{6}{8}$ **b** $\dfrac{3}{12}$ **c** $\dfrac{2}{6}$ **d** $\dfrac{5}{15}$

   e $\dfrac{4}{12}$ **f** $\dfrac{2}{8}$ **g** $\dfrac{6}{9}$ **h** $\dfrac{4}{10}$

3 a Write each fraction in its simplest form.

   i $\dfrac{2}{10}$ **ii** $\dfrac{5}{45}$ **iii** $\dfrac{20}{30}$ **iv** $\dfrac{40}{55}$

   v $\dfrac{15}{25}$ **vi** $\dfrac{27}{81}$ **vii** $\dfrac{14}{49}$ **viii** $\dfrac{48}{64}$

  b Copy and complete these equivalent fractions.

   i $\dfrac{1}{2} = \dfrac{\square}{16}$ **ii** $\dfrac{6}{7} = \dfrac{24}{\square}$ **iii** $\dfrac{5}{9} = \dfrac{\square}{81}$

   iv $\dfrac{6}{13} = \dfrac{\square}{65}$ **v** $\dfrac{24}{32} = \dfrac{6}{\square}$ **vi** $\dfrac{5}{75} = \dfrac{1}{\square}$

4 Convert these fractions to

  a improper fractions

   i $4\dfrac{3}{5}$ **ii** $6\dfrac{3}{7}$ **iii** $9\dfrac{1}{2}$ **iv** $5\dfrac{4}{5}$

   v $5\dfrac{3}{4}$ **vi** $10\dfrac{6}{9}$ **vii** $3\dfrac{2}{11}$ **viii** $12\dfrac{3}{5}$

  b mixed numbers.

   i $\dfrac{6}{5}$ **ii** $\dfrac{9}{4}$ **iii** $\dfrac{12}{5}$ **iv** $\dfrac{7}{4}$

   v $\dfrac{13}{7}$ **vi** $\dfrac{16}{5}$ **vii** $\dfrac{17}{5}$ **viii** $\dfrac{21}{4}$

5 Convert these fractions to decimals without using a calculator.

   a $\dfrac{6}{10}$ **b** $\dfrac{1}{4}$ **c** $\dfrac{10}{25}$

   d $\dfrac{34}{50}$ **e** $\dfrac{9}{10}$ **f** $\dfrac{22}{200}$

$\bigcirc$ Q 1016, 1019, 1042, 1075   **SEARCH**

Fractions and percentages

1 **a** There are 34 people on a bus. 16 are male and the rest are female.
   What fraction of the people on the bus are
   i   male   ii   female?

   b Manjit earns £450 a week. She pays £110 of her money
   in tax. She saves £90 each week. The rest she spends. What fraction
   of her weekly wage does Manjit
   i   pay in tax   ii   save   iii   spend?

   c Rhiannon has 13 pairs of trousers, 2 skirts, 25 tops and 9 pairs of
   shoes. What fraction of her clothes are
   i   trousers   ii   tops   iii   skirts?

2 Use a suitable method to calculate

   a $\frac{3}{11}$ of £33   **b** $\frac{5}{7}$ of 350 kg   **c** $\frac{7}{9}$ of 63p

   d $\frac{11}{20}$ of 100 g   **e** $\frac{9}{15}$ of 45°   **f** $\frac{14}{25}$ of €600

   g $\frac{5}{6}$ of $300   **h** $\frac{6}{13}$ of £104   **i** $\frac{1}{6}$ of 192 people

   j $\frac{1}{20}$ of 500 people   **k** $\frac{7}{12}$ of 168 cm   **l** $\frac{9}{11}$ of 572 miles.

3 **a** Find these percentages without using a calculator. You must show all
   the steps of your working.
   i   50% of £400   ii   25% of £200   iii   10% of £60
   iv   1% of 600p   v   30% of €550   vi   20% of $350
   vii   40% of 90p   viii 15% of $800   ix   55% of 1800 g
   x   75% of 860 kg   xi   35% of €180   xii   13% of 40 cm

   b Use a suitable method to calculate these. Where
   appropriate round your answers to 2 decimal places.
   i   25% of £49   ii   17.5% of 67 m   iii   34% of $458
   iv   12% of 740 tonne v   98% of 58 kg   vi   89% of 2550 mm
   vii   135% of 135 km   viii 7% of 95 m

4 In a packet of 25 biscuits, 12 are milk chocolate and the rest are plain
chocolate. What percentage are plain chocolate?

Calculations with fractions

1 Calculate each of these, leaving your answer in its simplest form, where appropriate.

a $\frac{1}{2} + \frac{1}{2}$

b $\frac{2}{7} + \frac{4}{7}$

c $\frac{10}{18} - \frac{4}{18}$

d $\frac{4}{15} + \frac{1}{15}$

e $\frac{23}{28} - \frac{2}{28}$

f $\frac{4}{54} + \frac{14}{54}$

2 Calculate these additions and subtractions, leaving your answer in its simplest form.

a $\frac{1}{4} + \frac{1}{8}$

b $\frac{3}{5} - \frac{3}{10}$

c $\frac{1}{3} - \frac{1}{6}$

d $\frac{2}{7} + \frac{3}{14}$

e $\frac{1}{5} + \frac{7}{10}$

f $\frac{4}{9} + \frac{1}{3}$

g $\frac{7}{4} - \frac{1}{5}$

h $\frac{4}{7} - \frac{1}{3}$

i $\frac{1}{7} + \frac{4}{5}$

3 Calculate these multiplications, leaving your answer in its simplest form.

a $3 \times \frac{2}{5}$

b $\frac{4}{5} \times 2$

c $\frac{4}{11} \times 3$

d $\frac{2}{7} \times \frac{7}{10}$

e $\frac{5}{8} \times \frac{5}{6}$

f $\frac{3}{11} \times \frac{1}{3}$

g $7 \times \frac{8}{9}$

h $\frac{5}{7} \times \frac{2}{3}$

i $\frac{9}{11} \times \frac{3}{5}$

j $3\frac{3}{4} \times 4$

k $1\frac{2}{3} \times 9$

l $1\frac{1}{2} \times 2\frac{3}{4}$

4 Calculate these divisions, leaving your answer in its simplest form.

a $5 \div \frac{7}{8}$

b $8 \div \frac{1}{9}$

c $9 \div \frac{3}{4}$

d $\frac{2}{5} \div 4$

e $\frac{3}{7} \div 3$

f $\frac{14}{13} \div \frac{3}{5}$

g $\frac{4}{7} \div \frac{1}{3}$

h $\frac{9}{11} \div \frac{3}{7}$

i $\frac{1}{2} \div \frac{6}{7}$

j $3\frac{3}{4} \div \frac{1}{3}$

k $\frac{8}{9} \div 1\frac{2}{3}$

l $3\frac{4}{5} \div 5\frac{1}{4}$

5 James spent $\frac{1}{5}$ of his pocket money on a cricket set. He spent $\frac{1}{3}$ of his pocket money on a football. Work out the fraction of his pocket money he has left.

Q 1017, 1040, 1046, 1047, 1074 **SEARCH**

5.4 Fractions, decimals and percentages

1 Write these percentages as **i** decimals **ii** fractions in their simplest form.
  a 42%   **b** 80%   **c** 90%   **d** 3%

2 Write each of these fractions as a percentage.
  a $\dfrac{45}{100}$ **b** $\dfrac{13}{50}$ **c** $\dfrac{4}{25}$

  d $\dfrac{7}{10}$ **e** $\dfrac{3}{5}$ **f** $\dfrac{3}{20}$

  g $\dfrac{46}{200}$ **h** $\dfrac{85}{500}$ **i** $\dfrac{45}{150}$

3 Change these fractions to decimals using a calculator.
Give your answers to a suitable degree of accuracy.
  a $\dfrac{13}{40}$ **b** $\dfrac{5}{8}$ **c** $\dfrac{12}{15}$

  d $\dfrac{3}{7}$ **e** $\dfrac{19}{21}$ **f** $\dfrac{12}{7}$

4 Write these decimals as **i** percentages **ii** fractions in their simplest form.
  a 0.2   **b** 0.7   **c** 0.45
  d 0.05   **e** 0.35   **f** 0.8
  g 0.32   **h** 0.525   **i** 0.71

5 Put these lists of numbers in order, from lowest to highest.
  a 5.21   2.56   5.02   5.19   2.5
  b 0.36   0.632   0.236   0.365   0.635
  c 3.54   4.26   3.504   3.453   3.624
  d 7.32   7.032   7.317   7.3   7.02

6 For each pair of fractions choose either < or > to show which fraction is greater.
  a $\dfrac{1}{4}$ $\dfrac{1}{5}$ **b** $\dfrac{9}{10}$ $\dfrac{9}{12}$ **c** $\dfrac{7}{10}$ $\dfrac{4}{5}$

  d $\dfrac{4}{5}$ $\dfrac{19}{25}$ **e** $\dfrac{5}{12}$ $\dfrac{1}{4}$ **f** $\dfrac{29}{100}$ $\dfrac{3}{10}$

7 Write these numbers in order of size from lowest to highest.
  a 0.5, 22%, $\dfrac{3}{10}$, 0.45, $\dfrac{2}{5}$ **b** $\dfrac{4}{7}$, 55%, $\dfrac{5}{11}$, 0.52, $\dfrac{1}{2}$

  c $\dfrac{7}{12}$, 62%, 0.54, $\dfrac{2}{3}$, 0.6   **d** $\dfrac{3}{4}$, $\dfrac{7}{9}$, 0.77, $\dfrac{7}{13}$, 80%

1 Write these decimals as fractions in their simplest form.

    a 0.2   **b** 0.8   **c** 0.45

    d 0.35   **e** 0.09   **f** 0.125

2 Simplify each fraction.

    a $\dfrac{2}{4}$ **b** $\dfrac{9}{12}$ **c** $\dfrac{20}{25}$ **d** $\dfrac{9}{27}$

    e $\dfrac{40}{32}$ **f** $\dfrac{54}{60}$ **g** $\dfrac{70}{110}$ **h** $\dfrac{45}{50}$

3 **a** Claire used 3000 letters in her essay. 35% of the letters were vowels. How many of the letters were vowels?

    b Amir earns £55 a week. He spends $\dfrac{7}{10}$ of what he earns. How much does he spend?

    c A tank can hold 140 litres when full. Water is poured into the tank until it is 65% full. How much water is in the tank?

4 Calculate each of these and leave your answer in its simplest form.

    a $\dfrac{1}{3} \times \dfrac{2}{5}$ **b** $\dfrac{3}{7} \times \dfrac{1}{3}$ **c** $\dfrac{9}{10} \times \dfrac{4}{5}$

    d $\dfrac{3}{4} \times \dfrac{7}{9}$ **e** $\dfrac{5}{7} \times \dfrac{1}{4}$ **f** $\dfrac{1}{2} \times \dfrac{5}{9}$

    g $\dfrac{2}{3} \div \dfrac{3}{5}$ **h** $\dfrac{3}{7} \div \dfrac{5}{6}$ **i** $\dfrac{5}{12} \div \dfrac{4}{5}$

    j $\dfrac{4}{5} \div \dfrac{2}{3}$ **k** $\dfrac{9}{10} \div \dfrac{1}{8}$ **l** $\dfrac{3}{5} \div \dfrac{3}{7}$

5 **a** Write these decimals as fractions in their simplest form.

    i 0.1   **ii** 0.08   **iii** 0.375

    b Convert these fractions to decimals without using a calculator.

    i $\dfrac{8}{10}$ **ii** $\dfrac{3}{4}$ **iii** $\dfrac{66}{300}$

    c Convert these fractions to decimals using a calculator. Give your answers to a suitable degree of accuracy.

    i $\dfrac{1}{13}$ **ii** $\dfrac{5}{9}$ **iii** $\dfrac{11}{17}$

6 Write these numbers in order of size from lowest to highest.

    a $\dfrac{1}{3}, \dfrac{3}{5}, 35\%, 0.3$ **b** $\dfrac{2}{3}, 60\%, 0.62, \dfrac{3}{7}$

    c $0.12, 24\%, \dfrac{1}{24}, \dfrac{1}{12}$ **d** $0.9, \dfrac{19}{20}, 0.89, \dfrac{11}{12}$

Substituting into formulae

1 Sonia worked out the cost of petrol used in her car.

| Cost of petrol in £ | = | Number of miles travelled | × | 0.15 |

a What is the cost of travelling one mile?

b Sonia needs to travel 150 miles. Work out the cost of the petrol used.

2 The formula $F = \dfrac{9C}{5} + 32$ is used to convert temperatures given in °C (Celsius) to °F (Fahrenheit).
Work out the temperature in Fahrenheit (F) when

a $C = 20$ **b** $C = -10$.

3 For each formula, work out the value of y when $a = 3$ and $b = -2$.

a $y = 5a - b$ **b** $y = 2a - 3b$ **c** $y = ab$

d $y = a^2 + b$ **e** $y = 2ab^2$ **f** $y = b^3$

g $y = 2a^2 + b$ **h** $y = 3a - b$ **i** $y = b - a$

4 The cost of hiring a cement mixer is £29 plus £5 per hour.

a Write a formula for how much it costs, C, to hire the cement mixer for n hours.

b Use your formula to work out how much it costs to hire a cement mixer for 8 hours.

5 The formula for the volume, V, of a cuboid is

$V = lwh$

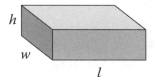

where l = length, w = width and h = height.

a Find the volume of a cuboid with $l = 5$ cm, $w = 2$ cm, $h = 3$ cm.

b Which of these cuboids will give the largest volume?

i $l = 4$ cm, $w = 5$ cm, $h = 2$ cm

ii $l = 4$ cm, $w = 3$ cm, $h = 3$ cm

iii $l = 5$ cm, $w = 1$ cm, $h = 7$ cm

Using standard formulae

1 Write down the inverse operation to these operations.

    a $+ 9$ **b** $- 7$ **c** $\times 10$ **d** $\div 4$

2 Copy and complete the input/output table for this function machine.

Input	Output
0	
1	
2	
3	
4	
	42

3 Draw a function machine like that in question **2** for each equation. Create an input/output table for each equation for inputs of 0, 1, 2, 3, 4; and use your machines to calculate the outputs.

    a $y = 4x + 5$ **b** $y = x + 10$ **c** $y = \dfrac{x}{2} + 6$

    d $y = x - 5$ **e** $y = \dfrac{x}{4} + 5$ **f** $y = -2x - 6$

4 Rearrange each formula to make a the subject.

    a $a + 4b = 10$ **b** $4a - b = 12$

    c $6b + a = 20$ **d** $b = \dfrac{a}{3} + 4$

    e $16 + 3a = 7b$

5 Jim's grandmother uses this formula for calculating the amount of cooking time, in hours, t, needed to roast a turkey

    $t = 0.5m + 2$

where m = mass of the turkey.

    a Rearrange the formula to make m the subject.

    b Using the rearranged formula, work out the mass of the turkey if Jim uses a cooking time, t, of

        i 3.5 hours

        ii 3 hours

        iii 5 hours.

Q 1159, 1171, 1940   **SEARCH**

Equations, identities and functions

1 Copy and complete the table. Choose from the words *identity, equation, inequality* or *formula* for the right-hand column. The first one has been completed for you.

	Identity, equation or formula?
$a \times a \times a \equiv a^3$	identity
$3x + 4 = 9x - 2$	
$4p^2(p - 1) \equiv 4p^3 - 4p^2$	
$A = \pi r^2$	
$x^2 = 49$	
$V = lwh$	
$6x \times 5 \geq 60$	

2 A cuboid has a square base of side length y cm. The height of the cuboid is $(y + 2)$ cm. The volume of the cuboid is 34 cm³. Show that $y^3 + 2y^2 = 34$.

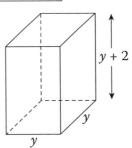

3 a Expand these expressions.

    i $4(p - 3)$ **ii** $5(7 - q)$

    iii $2(4r + 3) + 3(r - 2)$ **iv** $5(3t - 2) - 4(t - 7)$

    v $7(u^2 - 3u + 2)$ **vi** $4(v^2 - 3v + 5) - 6(v^2 + 3v - 2)$

b Factorise these expressions.

    i $2w - 6$ **ii** $18x + 54$ **iii** $15yz + 25z$ **iv** $6a^2 - 15$

c Expand and then factorise this expression.

     $2(b - 6) + 4(b - 4)$

4 A cylinder has volume $\pi r^2 h$ and a curved surface area of $2\pi rh$, where r is the radius of the base and h is the height of the cylinder.

A cone with the same radius and height has volume $\frac{1}{3}\pi r^2 h$ and curved surface area πrl, where l is the slant height.

A pillar consists of this cone on top of the cylinder.

a Show that the volume of the pillar is given by the formula
$$V = \frac{4}{3}\pi r^2 h.$$

b Find, and simplify, a formula for the curved surface area of the pillar.

5 a Show, by substituting some numbers of your own, that the square of one number subtracted from the square of a bigger number is the same as the sum of the numbers multiplied by the difference between them.

b By expanding the expression $(a + b)(a - b)$ prove that part **a** is true for all numbers.

c Without using a calculator, find the value of $97.5^2 - 2.5^2$.

Use your calculator to check your answer.

4 Expanding and factorising 2

1 Expand and simplify these expressions.

a $(x + 3)(x + 4)$ **b** $(y + 4)(y - 1)$

c $(3 + p)^2$ **d** $(x + 5)(x - 5)$

e $(h - 5)(h + 2)$ **f** $(2x + 3)(x + 5)$

g $(3t + 1)(2t + 5)$ **h** $(3m + 4)^2$

i $(3p + q)(2p - 3q)$ **j** $(4x - 3y)^2$

2 Factorise these expressions.

a $(a + b) + 3(a + b)^2$ **b** $(p + qr)^2 - 6(p + qr)$

c $pq + rq + px + rx$ **d** $xy + xw - 2y - 2w$

3 Use factorisation to help you evaluate these without using a calculator.

a $3 \times 0.43 + 3 \times 1.57$

b $5 \times 4.93 - 5 \times 2.73$

c $4.78^2 + 4.78 \times 5.22$

4 Factorise each of these expressions using double brackets.

a $x^2 + 7x + 12$ **b** $x^2 + 6x - 16$

c $x^2 - 4x - 45$ **d** $x^2 - 11x + 28$

e $x^2 - 8x + 16$ **f** $x^2 - 49$

g $x^2 - 2x - 120$ **h** $x^2 - 196$

5 **a** Show clearly that $(x - y)(x + y) \equiv x^2 - y^2$.

     b Hence, without using a calculator, evaluate $5.1^2 - 4.9^2$.
You **must** show your workings.

6 Factorise completely these quadratic expressions.

a $x^2 + 6x + 5$ **b** $x^2 + 7x - 18$

c $x^2 - 3x - 18$ **d** $x^2 - 15x - 100$

e $x^2 - 21x + 110$ **f** $x^2 - 16x + 64$

1 Teresa's sweets cost 6p each.
A packet of crisps costs 25p.

   a Write a formula for the total cost of n sweets and c packets of crisps.

   b If $n = 20$ and $c = 3$, use your formula to work out the total cost of sweets and crisps.

2 Whilst doing a science experiment, Michelle is told to use the formula $v = 9.91t + 5.45$ to work out the value of v.

She uses her calculator to work out the value of v when $t = 6.78$.

   a Work out the correct value of v when $t = 6.78$.

When $t = 8.26$ Michelle works out the answer to be 87.3066.
Michelle's answer is correct.
Michelle's friend Leah worked out v to be 23.62 when $t = 8.26$.

   b Suggest what is the most likely error made by Leah.

3 The voltage, V, in an electrical circuit with current, I, and resistance, R, is given by the formula $V = IR$.

   a What is V when   **i** $I = 6$ and $R = 8$ **ii** $I = 8$ and $R = 12$?

   b What is R when $V = 56$ and $I = 8$?

4 Rearrange these formulae to make a the subject.

   a $a + 3b = 12$ **b** $2a - 3b = 15$ **c** $8b + a = 24$

   d $b = \dfrac{a}{5} - 5$ **e** $15 - 3a = 6b$

5 **a** Expand, simplify and then factorise the following expressions.

     i $4(e - 6) + 12$ **ii** $3(q + 4) + 2q - 2$ **iii** $2(6g - 7) - 3(2g - 2)$

   b Explain why these statements are **not** identities.

     i $3a$ and a^3 **ii** $2(a + 1)$ and $a^2 + 2$

     iii $\dfrac{3a + 6}{3}$ and $3a + 2$ **iv** $(4a)^2$ and $16a$

6 Factorise these expressions.

   a $x^2 + 8x + 7$ **b** $x^2 + 5x - 24$ **c** $x^2 - 5x + 4$

   d $x^2 - 5x - 24$ **e** $y^2 - y - 12$ **f** $x^2 - 3x - 18$

   g $x^2 + 4x - 12$ **h** $x^2 - 2x - 35$

Measuring lengths and angles

1 Measure these lines
   i in millimetres   **ii** in centimetres.

   a _____

   b _____

   c _____

2 Measure and calculate the perimeter of these shapes in
   i cm   **ii** mm.

   a 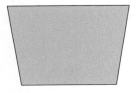   **b**

3 Measure each of these angles and state what type of angle it is.

   a   **b**

   c    **d**

4 The scale of a map is $1:5\,000\,000$.
   a How many km does 1 cm represent?
   b How many cm represent 14.5 km?
   c How many km are represented by 8.5 cm?

5 Why would a scale $1:6\,000\,000$ not be appropriate if Max wants to do a scale drawing of his house? Suggest a more appropriate scale, explaining your answer carefully.

7.2 Area of a 2D shape

1 Find the area of each triangle.
State the units of your answers.

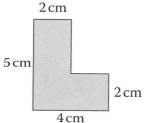

a 10 mm, 13 mm

b 6 cm, 8 cm

c 3 m

2 Find the area of these shapes.
State the units of your answers.

a

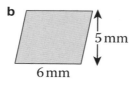

2 cm, 5 cm, 2 cm, 4 cm

b

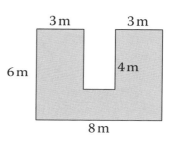

3 m, 3 m, 6 m, 4 m, 8 m

3 Find the area of these shapes. State the units.

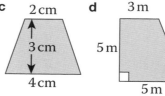

a 3 cm, 4 cm

b 5 mm, 6 mm

c 2 cm, 3 cm, 4 cm

d 3 m, 5 m, 5 m

4 The area of each shape is given. Find the unknown length.

a

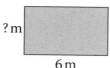

? m, 6 m
Area = 24 m²

b

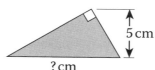

5 cm, ? cm
Area = 40 cm²

c

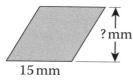

? mm, 15 mm
Area = 3.75 cm²

d

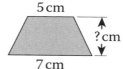

5 cm, ? cm, 7 cm
Area = 48 cm²

Q 1108, 1128, 1129 **SEARCH**

Transformations I

1 Copy and complete the diagrams to show the reflections of the shapes in the mirror lines.

a 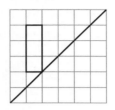 **b** 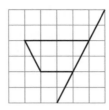 **c**

2 State the angle and direction for each of these rotations. The shaded shape is the starting position.

a   **b**   **c**   **d**

3 Describe these transformations.

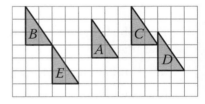

   a *A* onto *B*   **b** *A* onto *C*

   c *B* onto *C*   **d** *B* onto *D*

   e *C* onto *D*   **f** *C* onto *E*

   g *D* onto *E*   **h** *D* onto *A*

4 Copy the shape and grid onto squared paper.

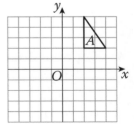

   a Reflect the triangle *A* in the *x*-axis. Label it *B*.

   b Rotate the triangle *B* by 90° clockwise about the origin. Label it *C*.

   c (**Challenge**) Describe the single transformation that maps triangle *A* onto triangle *C*.

5 Copy the grid and enlarge the triangle by scale factor 2 through the centre of enlargement *O*.

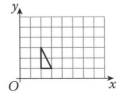

7.4 Transformations 2

Use square grid paper for the enlargements on this page.

1 Copy each diagram onto squared paper. Enlarge each shape by the given scale factor using the dot as the centre of enlargement.

   a scale factor 3   **b** scale factor $\frac{1}{2}$ **c** scale factor 2

  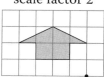

2 Copy each diagram. Find the centre of enlargement and calculate the scale factor for these enlargements. The shaded shape is the original shape.

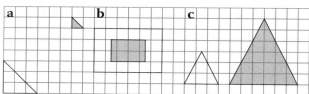

3 Describe fully the single transformation that maps

   a trapezium X onto trapezium Y

   b trapezium Y onto trapezium X.

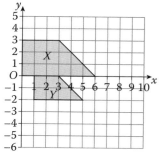

4 Copy this diagram.

   a Reflect $ABCD$ in the x-axis, and label the image $A'B'C'D'$.

   b Rotate $A'B'C'D'$ by $180°$ about the origin, and label the image $A''B''C''D''$.

   c Find the single transformation that maps $ABCD$ to $A''B''C''D''$.

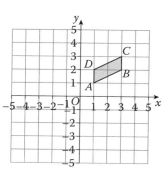

Q 1125   **SEARCH**

1 Calculate the area of each shape. State the units.

a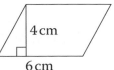
4 cm
6 cm

b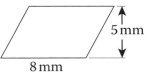
5 mm
8 mm

c
3 cm
4 cm
5 cm

2 Copy the grid onto squared paper.

   a Reflect triangle A in the y-axis and label it B.

   b Translate triangle B by $\begin{pmatrix} 1 \\ 5 \end{pmatrix}$ and label it C.

   c Rotate triangle C through the origin $(0, 0)$ by $90°$ anticlockwise and label it D.

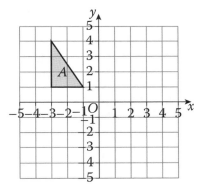

3 Copy this diagram.

   a Enlarge triangle X by scale factor 2, centre $(1, 2)$. Label the image Y.

   b Write the area of
     i triangle X
     ii triangle Y.

   c How many times larger than the area of triangle X is the area of triangle Y?

   d Enlarge triangle X by scale factor $\frac{1}{2}$, centre $(-3, 2)$. Label the image Z.

   e Write the area of
     i triangle X
     ii triangle Z.

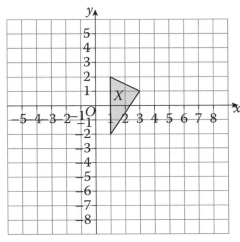

8.1 Probability experiments

1 Use the words ┃impossible┃, ┃unlikely┃, ┃even chance┃, ┃likely┃ or ┃certain┃ to describe these outcomes.

a You will get an even number when you roll an ordinary dice.

b It will snow in winter.

c It will rain during July.

d You will have a birthday this year.

e There are 32 days in December.

f You will pick a white ball from a bag containing 8 black and 8 white balls.

g You will spin an even number on a spinner with the numbers 2, 3, 4, 5, 6.

h You will pick a milk chocolate sweet from a bag containing 5 milk chocolates and 7 plain chocolates.

2 You roll a biased dice 150 times. The table shows the outcomes.

Score	1	2	3	4	5	6
Frequency	50	24	22	20	26	8

If you roll the dice once more, estimate the probability that it will land on a

a 1 **b** 6 **c** 2 or 5.

3 Cameron carries out a survey about the words in a book. He chooses a page at random and counts the letters in the first 150 words on that page. The table shows the outcomes of his experiment.

Number of letters	1	2	3	4	5	6	7	8
Frequency	8	14	35	45	30	10	5	3

The book has 30 000 words.
Estimate the number of 3-letter words in the book.

Q 1209, 1210, 1211   **SEARCH**

Expected outcomes

1 Claire throws a fair coin. She gets a tail.
Sonia then throws the same coin.

   a What is the probability that Sonia will get a tail?

   b Sonia throws the coin 40 times. Explain why she
may not get exactly 20 heads and 20 tails.

2 If you roll a fair dice 300 times, how many times would
you expect it to land on

   a a 6   **b** an even number

   c a factor of 8   **d** an 8?

3 Suzanne decides to roll a biased dice 500 times.
The probability that the dice will land on a six is 0.45.

   Work out an estimate for the number of times that the
dice will land on a six.

4 Freya carries out a statistical experiment. She throws a dice 120 times.
She scores a three 40 times.

   Is the dice fair? Explain your answer.

5 A dice is rolled 30 times in order to test its fairness.
The results of this experiment are shown below.

1	3	3	5	6	2	4	4	5	2
4	2	1	4	5	1	6	4	4	4
2	3	5	4	6	4	1	5	6	4

   a Work out the relative frequency of rolling each number.
   b Is the dice biased? Explain your answer.
   c What could you do to improve the experiment?

6 Jordan can't decide where to get married.
She writes the names of 25 locations on individual cards,
numbered 1 to 25, and puts them in a bag.

   a What is the probability that a card, drawn at random, will be
     i a multiple of 5   **ii** a prime number   **iii** a factor of 24?
   b What is the probability that a card, drawn at random, will not
     i have a 1 in it   **ii** be a square number?

Theoretical probability

1 A bag of sweets contains these flavours
4 strawberry   3 orange   2 blackcurrant   5 lemon.
Calculate the probability of picking

a   an orange sweet   **b**   a lemon sweet

c   a blackcurrant sweet   **d**   a raspberry sweet.

2 A pack of 52 playing cards contains four 'suits' which consist of 13 spades, 13 clubs, 13 hearts and 13 diamonds.
Each suit has cards numbered 2, 3, 4, 5, 6, 7, 8, 9, 10, Jack, Queen, King, Ace.
If you choose a card at random from the pack, what is the probability it will be

a   a heart

b   a Queen

c   a Queen of diamonds

d   a 2

e   an odd number spade

f   a Jack, Queen or King?

3 A box of chocolates contains milk and plain chocolates. Some of these chocolates contain nuts. The two-way table shows the number of chocolates in each category.

	Milk chocolate	**Plain chocolate**
Contains nuts	5	7
Does not contain nuts	12	8

You select one chocolate at random.

Calculate the probability that the chocolate is a

a   plain chocolate that contains nuts   **b**   milk chocolate

c   chocolate that contains nuts   **d**   plain chocolate

e   milk chocolate that contains nuts.

Q 1210, 1264   **SEARCH**

Mutually exclusive events

1 The probability that Lutterworth Hockey Team win each game is $\frac{7}{8}$.

    a Calculate the probability that they will lose a game.

    b If they play 24 games, how many games do you expect them to lose?

2 Richard has a bag of sweets. He picks one sweet out at random. The probability that the sweet is a particular colour is

Colour	Red	Green	Yellow	Orange	Purple
Probability	$\frac{1}{5}$	$\frac{1}{20}$	$\frac{3}{10}$	$\frac{15}{100}$	

    a Calculate the probability of picking a sweet that is

        i purple   **ii** blue.

    b If there are 40 sweets in the bag, how many of them are each colour?

3 The possible outcomes in a football match are win, lose or draw. The probability that Fowey Town Football Club win, lose or draw is shown in this table.

Outcome	Win	Lose	Draw
Probability	0.65	0.25	

    a Calculate the probability that Fowey Town will draw.

    b What is the most likely outcome?

4 The probability of Zahir being early or on time for work is 0.76.

    a Calculate the probability of his being late for work.

    b Over 300 work days, how many times would you expect him to be late for work?

5 The probability that a new car is faulty is 0.09. Calculate the probability that it is not faulty.

6 The probability of rain in Derby on Tuesday is 0.65. What is the probability that Tuesday in Derby will be dry?

1 The letters of the word MATHEMATICS are put into a bag. One letter is taken out at random.
Calculate the probability that the letter is

   a an M   **b** not an M   **c** a vowel
   d a consonant   **e** not an A   **f** a B.

2 A group of 40 students listened to three pieces of classical music and then noted their preferred piece. The table shows this information.

	Bach	Chopin	Debussy	Total
Male		6		18
Female	4			
Total		14	12	40

   a Copy and complete the table.
   b One student is chosen at random. Find the probability that the student
      i is female
      ii prefers Debussy
      iii is male and prefers Chopin.

   c These 40 students were a random sample selected from a year group of 140 students. How many of the year group would you expect
      i to prefer Bach   **ii** to be male?

3 Emma throws an ordinary fair dice once.

   a Write down the probability of the dice landing on
      i a four   **ii** an odd number.

   Emma throws a second fair dice once.
   The probability that this dice will land on each of the numbers 1 to 6 is given in the table.

Number	1	2	3	4	5	6
Probability		0.2	0.3	0.1	0.2	0.1

   b Find the probability of the dice landing on a 1.
   c Find the probability that the dice will land on a number higher than 4.

Estimation and approximation

1 Use rounding to estimate answers to these calculations.
Show how you rounded the numbers.

a $56 + 182$ **b** $598 - 86$ **c** $1348 + 67$

d $1504 - 497$ **e** $4355 + 897$

2 Give a suitable estimate for these calculations.
Show your workings clearly.

a 6.95×3.21 **b** $19.7 \div 4.3$

c $\dfrac{3.67 \times 5.24}{4.87}$ **d** $\dfrac{47.9 \times 32.1}{15.4}$

3 Estimate the answer to these calculations.

a $\dfrac{2.75 \times 6.3}{8.8}$ **b** $\dfrac{11.7 - 7.6}{1.7 + 6.25}$

4 Write a suitable estimate for each of these calculations.
In each case clearly show how you obtained your estimate.

a $21.5 + 23.5$ **b** $578 - 215$ **c** 2.98×5.05

d $19.75 \div 3.76$ **e** 49.98×4.87 **f** $86.7 \div 2.85$

g $\dfrac{5.6 \times 9.7}{3.87}$ **h** $\dfrac{29.7 \times 21.3}{39.6}$ **i** $\dfrac{29.55 \times 21.4^2}{6.1}$

5 Write a suitable estimate for each of these calculations. In each case clearly show how you obtained your estimate.

a $\dfrac{39.9 \times 21.5}{1.98^3}$

b $\dfrac{47.9 \times 9.8^2}{0.49 \times 21.56}$

c $\sqrt{98.7 \div 1.98}$

d $\{2.6^2 + (4.57 - 0.62)\}^2$

e $\dfrac{219 + (3.98 + 16.08)^2}{\sqrt{74.5 \div 2.11}}$

Calculator methods

1 Monique goes to the shops and buys

> 5 kg of potatoes at £0.45 per kg
> 1.54 kg of apples at £1.99 per kg
> 0.5 kg of tomatoes at £0.88 per kg
> 2.2 kg of bananas at £0.85 per kg
> 1.5 kg of carrots at £0.68 per kg
> 0.785 kg of cherries at £8.99 per kg
> 0.61 kg of grapes at £1.87 per kg
> 4 avocados at £0.67 each

  a Work out the total cost of the shopping.

  b Work out the change she would receive from a £20 note.

2 Use BIDMAS to work these out.

  a $8 \times 9 + 5$ **b** $12 \div 4 \times 3$

  c $12 \times (17 - 5)$ **d** $3 \times 5 + 6 \times 4$

  e $8 \times (9 - 3) \times 2$ **f** $6^2 + 15 \div 3$

  g $\dfrac{5 \times (4^2 - 2)}{7}$ **h** $\sqrt{120 - 2^3 \times 7}$

3 **a** Estimate the value of

     $\dfrac{19.6 \times 21.3}{(9.6)^2}$

  b Use your calculator to work out the exact value giving your answer to 2 decimal places.

4 Use your calculator to work out each of these. Write all the figures on your calculator display.

  a $\dfrac{6.53^2 \times 2.19 + 7.34}{5.13 - 3.78}$ **b** $\dfrac{94.39 - (4.8 + 2.71)^2}{5.81^2 - 5.42}$

5 Use a calculator to calculate these quantities.

  a $\left(4\dfrac{4}{5}\right)^2$ **b** 2^8 **c** $\sqrt{\dfrac{4}{9}}$ **d** $\sqrt[5]{243}$

.3 Measures and accuracy

1 Find the missing lengths. Give the units of your answers.

a

? cm

3 cm | Area = 36 cm²

b

? cm

2.5 cm | Area = 7.5 mm²

2 Convert these measurements to the units given.

a 30 mm = ___ cm   **b** 300 cm = ___ m

c 3 kg = ___ g   **d** 5000 ml = ___ litres

e 0.5 km = ___ m   **f** 6 litres = ___ ml

g 4.5 tonne = ___ kg   **h** 7 m = ___ cm

i 30 cl = ___ litres   **j** 0.25 cm = ___ mm

3 Jonathan took measurements around his school.
Are these values sensible?

a The height of the cherry tree outside the Maths building = 4.5 m.

b The mass of an apple from the school canteen = 1.6 kg.

c The height of the door into the French room = 215 cm.

d The capacity of the sink in the wash room = 2.3 litres.

4 These masses are given to the nearest kilogram. Give the lowest and highest masses they could represent.

a 3 kg   **b** 8 kg   **c** 15 kg   **d** 50 kg   **e** 0 kg

5 A pencil is of length 12 cm, measured to the nearest centimetre.
A pencil case is of length 12.1 cm, measured to the nearest millimetre.
Explain why it might not be possible for the pencil to fit in the pencil case.

6 Use the formula average speed = $\dfrac{\text{distance}}{\text{time}}$ to find the speed in km per hour of a car that travels 25 km in 20 minutes.

1 Write a suitable estimate for each calculation. Clearly show how you obtained your estimate.

a $31.5 + 53.5$ b $778 - 615$

c 3.98×6.15 d $29.85 \div 4.76$

e 79.98×4.21 f $99.7 \div 5.15$

g $\dfrac{9.6 \times 4.7}{5.13}$ h $\dfrac{69.7 \times 46.3}{19.6}$

i $\dfrac{56.55 \times 3.14^2}{6.1}$ j $\dfrac{(19.3 \times 1.98) + 9.8^2}{7.15}$

2 a Estimate the value of
$$\frac{89.4 \times 34.5}{1.92 \times 30.4}.$$

b Use your calculator to work out the value of
$$\frac{12.35 \times (3.4 + 4.9)}{2.4^2 \times 1.3}.$$

Give your answer to 2 decimal places.

3 Use your calculator to work out
$$(2.4^2 + 1.9) \times 2.38.$$

a Write all the figures shown on your calculator display.

b Round the answer in part **a** to 2 decimal places.

4 Steve is an electrician and he charges £49.50 as a call out charge and then £22.25 for each hour he works. How much does he get for 3.5 hours work?

5 Rupert decides to send a red rose to his girlfriend. The rose measures 30 cm, to the nearest centimetre. Rupert buys a presentation box of length 30.1 cm, measured to the nearest millimetre.

a Explain why the rose may not fit inside the box.

b What is the maximum length that Rupert may have to cut from the stem of the rose in order to make it fit in the box?

Solving linear equations 1

1 Solve these equations.

   a $x + 4 = 8$ **b** $x - 6 = -1$ **c** $x + 7 = 11$

   d $x - 7 = -2$ **e** $10 + x = 12$ **f** $8 - x = 5$

   g $14 - x = -1$ **h** $17 + x = 15$

2 **a** Write an equation for each of these.

   i a number added to 7 equals 19

   ii a number subtracted from 10 equals 3

   iii when subtracting 4 from a number you get 12

   iv a number added to 8 equals 2

   v a number added to −2 makes 1

   b Solve each of your equations.

3 Solve these equations.

   a $3x = 12$ **b** $4x = 20$ **c** $\dfrac{x}{3} = 5$

   d $20 = 10x$ **e** $\dfrac{x}{6} = 4$ **f** $\dfrac{h}{6} = 4$

   g $5x = -10$ **h** $\dfrac{t}{2} = 15$ **i** $2x = -6$

4 Solve these equations.

   a $x + 5 = 13$ **b** $\dfrac{x}{4} = 12$ **c** $20 - x = 19$

   d $3x = 15$ **e** $x + 5 = 4$ **f** $\dfrac{20}{x} = 2$

   g $10 + x = 12$ **h** $15 - x = 16$

5 Solve these equations.

   a $3b + 4 = 13$ **b** $6f - 3 = 9$ **c** $4f + 2 = 22$

   d $\dfrac{p}{3} + 3 = 7$ **e** $5m - 3 = 22$ **f** $\dfrac{r}{4} - 5 = 0$

   g $4d + 6 = 38$ **h** $4r - 10 = -2$ **i** $6k + 4 = 19$

   j $6t + 5 = -13$ **k** $\dfrac{f}{3} + 4 = 1$ **l** $9p - 4 = -31$

6 The diagram shows a square with sides $4y + 3$.

   a Write an expression for the perimeter of the square.

   b The perimeter of the square is 108 cm.
   Find the value of y.

$4y + 3$

10.2 Solving linear equations 2

1 Solve these equations.

   a $3(x + 5) = 24$ **b** $5(x - 2) = 35$ **c** $4(10 - x) = 28$

   d $-2(x + 5) = -20$ **e** $4(x + 4) = 8$ **f** $7(2x + 4) = 4$

   g $3x + 2 = 6x - 2$ **h** $5x - 3 = 3x + 3$ **i** $9x + 4 = 12x - 11$

   j $3x + 7 = 5x + 4$ **k** $7x - 4 = 3x - 21$ **l** $2x - 4 = 5x + 3.5$

2 Solve the equations.

   a $2x + 3 = 15$ **b** $5a + 7 = 42$ **c** $4m + 5 = 9$

   d $7p + 4 = 18$ **e** $2(x + 1) = 12$ **f** $4(2a + 2) = 32$

   g $12w - 7 = 10w - 1$ **h** $3(2m - 1) = 5(m + 1)$

3 Solve these equations.

   a $2(b + 1) = 3b - 22$ **b** $5(f - 2) = 4(f + 1)$

   c $2(k + 1) = 3k - 41$ **d** $4(u - 2) = 2(u + 10)$

   e $4(v + 1) = 6v - 44$ **f** $3(x + 5) = 2x + 19$

   g $5y - 10 = -4(y + 7)$ **h** $5(2x + 4) = 5(4x + 1)$

4 Solve these equations.

   a $\dfrac{x + 3}{2} = 4$ **b** $\dfrac{x + 3}{5} = 4$

   c $\dfrac{3x - 6}{2} = 4.5$ **d** $\dfrac{3x - 6}{6} = 4.5$

   e $\dfrac{10 - x}{2} = 3$ **f** $\dfrac{12 - 2x}{2} = 1$

   g $\dfrac{3x + 2}{2} = 4$ **h** $\dfrac{5x + 2}{2} = -2$

   i $\dfrac{3x - 4}{13} = 2$ **j** $\dfrac{5 - 3x}{7} = 2$

5 The diagram shows a rectangle of side lengths $2x - 3$ and 5.

   a   Write an expression for the area of the rectangle.

   b   The area of the rectangle is $45\,\text{cm}^2$.
       Find the value of x.

5

$2x - 3$

Quadratic equations

1 Solve these quadratic equations by factorising.

a $x^2 + 6x + 8 = 0$ **b** $x^2 + 11x + 24 = 0$ **c** $x^2 + 5x - 6 = 0$

d $x^2 + 6x - 16 = 0$ **e** $x^2 = 9x - 20$ **f** $x^2 + 7 = 8x$

g $x^2 - 4x = 0$ **h** $2x^2 + 12x = 0$

Hint: Parts **g** and **h** factorise into single brackets.

2 Solve these quadratic equations.

a $x^2 + 7x + 12 = 0$ **b** $x^2 + 9x + 14 = 0$ **c** $x^2 + 4x - 5 = 0$

d $x^2 - 14x + 40 = 0$ **e** $x^2 = 5x - 24$ **f** $x^2 - 9x = 0$

3 This is the graph of $y = x^2 - 2x$.

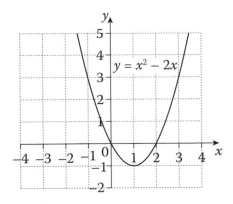

Use the graph to find approximate solutions, to 1 decimal place where appropriate, for these equations.

a $x^2 - 2x = 0$ **b** $x^2 - 2x = 3$

c $x^2 - 2x = 2$ **d** $x^2 - 2x = -1$

1 Solve these simultaneous equations by either adding or subtracting to eliminate one variable.

a $x + 2y = 7$
$x + y = 4$

b $5x + 2y = 8$
$2x + 2y = 2$

c $p - 3q = 10$
$4p + 3q = 10$

d $a = 5b + 8$
$3b = 8 - a$

2 Solve these simultaneous equations by the elimination method.

a $3x + y = 11$
$2x + 2y = 10$

b $4x - y = 9$
$3x + 2y = 4$

c $5a + 3b = 19$
$3a - 2b = 19$

3 Solve these simultaneous equations algebraically.

a $x + y = 6$
$2x - y = 9$

b $2x + y = 3$
$3x + 3y = 3$

c $2x - 3y = 2$
$5x + 2y = 24$

4 **a** Copy and complete the table to generate three coordinates for the line graph $y = 3x - 1$.

x	−1	0	1
y		−1	

b Draw an x-axis from −2 to 2 and a y-axis from −5 to 5.
Plot the graph of $y = 3x - 1$ on your axes.

c Plot the graph of $y = 3 - x$ on the same set of axes.

d Use your graphs to solve the simultaneous equations
$$y = 3x - 1$$
$$y = 3 - x.$$

5 Here are my receipts from two visits to 'Café Connection'.

By setting up a pair of simultaneous equations work out the cost of a latte.

2 Lattes
3 Carrot cakes
£5.85

1 Carrot cake
2 Lattes
£3.95

.5   Inequalities

1   In these inequalities y is an integer.
List all possible values of y that satisfy these inequalities.

a $-3 < y < -1$

b $-5\, y < 2$

c $4 > y > 1$

d $6 < 2y < 10$

e $-4 < 4y \leq 16$

2   **a**   List all the possible values of x that satisfy this inequality where x is an integer.

$-3 < x \leq 1$

b   Show all the possible values of x on a number line.

3   Solve these inequalities and show the solution set on a number line.

a $3x \leq 9$ **b** $4x > 16$ **c** $5x \geq 15$

d $6x \leq 18$ **e** $3x \leq -12$ **f** $2x \geq -20$

4   Solve these inequalities and show the solution set on a number line.

a $4x + 5 > 17$ **b** $3x - 4 < 5$ **c** $3x + 1 < -2$

d $5x + 3 \leq 23$ **e** $3x + 5 \geq 20$ **f** $6x + 2 < -16$

5   Solve these inequalities and show the solution set on a number line.

a $5x + 3 > 13$ **b** $8x - 4 < 0$ **c** $4x + 1 < -11$

d $6x - 3 \leq 21$ **e** $2x + 5 \geq 22$ **f** $10x + 2 < -3$

6   Solve these linear inequalities.

a $2(x + 4) < 20$ **b** $3(x - 3) > 16$ **c** $4(x + 1) > 30$

d $5(x - 2) \leq 40$ **e** $36 \leq 3(x + 2)$ **f** $-10 \leq 5(y - 3)$

1 Solve these equations.

    a $4n - 6 = 34$ **b** $4f + 3 = -17$

    c $10 = 3x + 1$ **d** $20 - 5x = -5$

    e $7d + 4 = -10$ **f** $24 - 5k = 9$

2 Solve these equations.

    a $\dfrac{x+4}{3} = 21$ **b** $3(5x - 6) = 147$

    c $\dfrac{2(x+6)}{3} = 6$ **d** $2x + 4 = 3x - 1$

    e $6(x + 1) = 14(x - 1)$ **f** $2(5x + 3) = 12x - 3$

3 Solve these quadratic equations by factorising.

    a $x^2 + 10x + 21 = 0$ **b** $a^2 + 4a - 45 = 0$

    c $b^2 - 5b - 36 = 0$ **d** $y^2 - 5y = 0$

    e $3t^2 + 12t = 0$

4 Solve these simultaneous equations algebraically.

    a $2p + 3q = 12$ **b** $5a + 3b = 7$ **c** $4x - y = 19$

        $p - q = 1$ $2a - 2b = 6$ $2x - 3y = 7$

5 The diagram shows the graphs of $y = x^2 - 2x - 3$, $y = 3$ and $y = -2$.

Use the graphs to find approximate solutions to these equations.

    a $x^2 - 2x - 3 = 3$

    b $x^2 - 2x - 3 = -2$

    c $x^2 - 2x - 3 = 0$

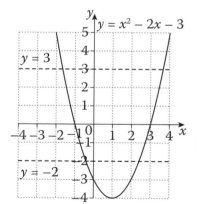

6 Solve these inequalities and show the solution set on a number line.

    a $3x + 6 > 0$ **b** $3x + 2 \geq 20$

    c $2(y + 3) > 12$ **d** $20 \leq 4(y + 1)$

1.1 Circles 1

1 **a** Draw a circle with a radius of 3 cm.

    b Draw a chord of length 4 cm inside the circle.

    c Shade this segment of the circle.

2 Work out the circumference of these circles. Use $\pi = 3.14$.

    a Diameter = 4 cm   **b** Diameter = 6.5 cm

    c Radius = 3 cm   **d** Radius = 2.5 cm

3 Calculate the area of these circles. State the units of your answers.

a 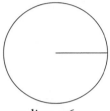   **b** 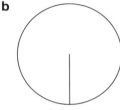   **c**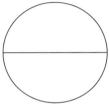

      radius = 6 cm   radius = 9 m   diameter = 36 mm

4 Using $\pi = 3.14$, calculate the radius of each circle.

    a Diameter = 6.3 cm

    b Circumference = 94.2 mm

    c Area = 50.24 cm^2

    d Area = 78.5 m^2

5 The diagram shows a semi-circle.

    The diameter of the semi-circle is 12 mm.

    Calculate

    a its area

    b its perimeter.

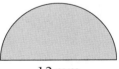

12 mm

Hint: A semi-circle is half a circle.

11.2 Circles 2

1 Find the area of each sector.

a
40° 16 mm

b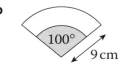
100° 9 cm

c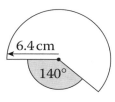
6.4 cm 140°

d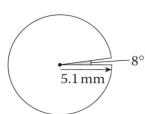
5.1 mm 8°

2 Find the perimeter of each of the sectors in question **1**.

3 Find each of the shaded angles.

a arc length = 4.2 cm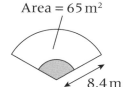
5 cm

b arc length = 24 m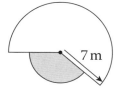
7 m

c Area = 65 m²
8.4 m

d arc length = 58.9 mm
75 mm

4 A circular flowerbed of radius 1.4 m is surrounded by a path of width 70 cm.

Find the area of the path.

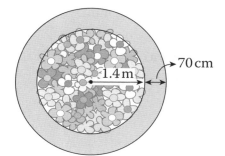
1.4 m 70 cm

.3 Constructions

1 **a** Draw a line *AB*, so that *AB* = 12 cm.

A ———————————•——————————— B
                    P

b Mark the point *P*, so that *AP* = 8 cm.

c Construct the perpendicular to *AB* that passes through point *P*.

2 **a** Using a pair of compasses construct the triangle *ABC*.

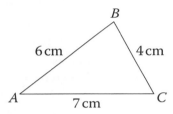

b Construct the perpendicular bisectors of *AB*, *BC* and *AC*.

c Label the point of intersection of the perpendicular bisectors as *O*.

d What do you notice about point *O*?

3 **a** Using a pair of compasses, construct the triangle *PQR*.

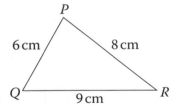

b Construct the angle bisectors for the angle *P*, angle *Q* and angle *R*.

c Label the point of intersection as *O*.

d Draw a circle, centre *O*, that just touches the lines *PQ*, *QR* and *PR*.

e State the radius of this circle.

4 Construct each of the following angles.

a 30°   **b** 60°   **c** 45°

1   Copy the line *AB* and draw the locus of the points that are always 2 cm from the line.

   A ――――――――――― *B*

2   Make an accurate copy of the points *A*, *B* and *C*.
   (You can use tracing paper.)

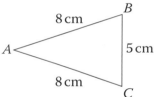

   A •

   •*C*

   B •

   Shade the region that satisfies all three of these conditions
   a   less than 2 cm from *A*   **b**   closer to *AB* than to *AC*
   c   closer to *A* than to *B*.

3   Construct an accurate drawing of this triangle.

```
            B
   8 cm    ╱|
          ╱ |
   A ◄────  | 5 cm
          ╲ |
   8 cm    ╲|
            C
```

4   The triangle in question **3** represents a triangular garden *ABC*.
   The scale of the diagram is 1 cm = 1 m.
   A gardener plans to build a pond in the garden so that it is
   a   within 4 m of point *C*
   b   equal distance from *AB* and *AC*.
   On your triangle that you constructed in question **3**, use a cross to show the possible location of the pond.

5   **a**   Trace this line and points marked *x* and *y*.

   x•

   •*y*

   b   Use a ruler and a pair of compasses to construct a perpendicular from the point *x to* the line.
   c   Use a ruler and a pair of compasses to construct a perpendicular from the point *y on* the line.

Q 1147   SEARCH

1 Calculate the **i** circumference **ii** area of each circle.

a 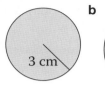 3 cm

b 5 cm

c 4.5 cm

d  3.2 cm

2 Jason has a lawn which is a rectangle with a semi-circle at each end. Calculate the area and perimeter of Jason's lawn.

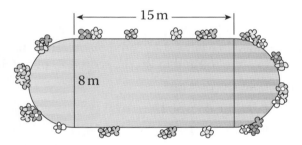
15 m

8 m

3 **a** Find the area of this sector. **b** Calculate the missing angle.

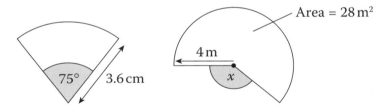
75° 3.6 cm

Area = 28 m²

4 m

x

4 **a** Draw a line 6 cm long and label it *AB*. Construct the perpendicular bisector of *AB* and label it *CD*. Label the point where these two lines meet as *X*.

 b Bisect the angle *CXB*. Label this new line *XY*.

 c What is the size of angle *CXY*?

5 **a** *A* and *B* are two points 8 cm apart. Draw the locus of points that are equidistant from *A* and *B*.

 b On the same diagram, draw the locus of points that are 3 cm from *A*.

12.1 Proportion

1 There are 700 students at Fowey School.

a 15% of these students were absent from school on Friday. Work out how many students were not absent on Friday.

b Carrie-Ann says that more than 255 of the 700 students were absent on Friday.

Is Carrie-Ann correct? Explain your answer.

c 56% of the students are girls.

Work out how many of the students are girls.

d 154 of the students are in Year 7.

Write 154 out of 700 as a percentage.

2 a Michelle took three tests. In Maths she scored 63 out of 72, in Science she scored 44 out of 60 and in RE she scored 29 out of 50.

i In which subject did she do best?

ii In which subject did she do worst?

b Leah took three different tests. In English she scored 58 out of 80, in Geography she scored 57 out of 72 and in PE she scored 51 out of 60.

i In which subject did she do best?

ii In which subject did she do worst?

3 Express each of these as proportions. Give your answer as a fraction in its simplest form.

a 50 kg as a fraction of 80 kg

b £20 as a proportion of £50

c 16 cm as a fraction of 64 cm

d 450 cm as a fraction of 600 cm

e 44 minutes as a proportion of 60 minutes

f 540 metres as a fraction of 4 metres

g 78p as a fraction of £2.

2.2 Ratio

1. Write these ratios in the form $1 : n$.

a	$3 : 9$	b	$4 : 16$	c	$5 : 10$	d	$7 : 21$
e	$10 : 25$	f	$15 : 60$	g	$4 : 28$	h	$6 : 54$
i	$22 : 33$	j	$18 : 24$	k	$27 : 45$	l	$36 : 48$

2. Work out each of these problems.
   a. Divide £30 in the ratio $1 : 4$.
   b. Divide £120 in the ratio $5 : 7$.
   c. Divide 84 kg in the ratio $2 : 5$.
   d. Divide 135p in the ratio $8 : 7$.
   e. Divide 105p in the ratio $5 : 2$.

3. a. A plank of wood 3.2 m long is divided into three pieces in the ratio $2 : 9 : 5$. How long is each piece of wood?

   b. The angles in a quadrilateral are in the ratio $1 : 2 : 4 : 5$. Calculate the size of the four angles.

   c. The ratio of membership of men and women at a golf club is $7 : 3$. If there are 660 members at the club, how many of them are women?

   d. Pete and Jo share £279.50 in the ratio $7 : 3$.
   How much does Pete receive?

4. Jack shares £180 between his two children Ruth and Ben.
   The ratio of Ruth's share to Ben's share is $5 : 4$.
   a. Work out how much each child is given.
   Ben then gives 10% of his share to Ruth.
   b. Work out the percentage of the £180 that Ruth now has.

5. a. Manjit cuts a piece of string into two pieces.
   Piece A is 12 cm long and piece B is 16 cm long.
   i. How many times longer is piece B compared to piece A?
   ii. What proportion of the length of piece B is piece A?

   b. James is 8 years old and his Auntie Claire is 32 years old.
   i. How many times older is Claire compared to James?
   ii. What proportion of Claire's age is James' age?

Percentage change

1   Find these percentage increases and decreases.

   a   Increase £30 by 10%   **b**   Decrease 150 m by 20%

   c   Decrease £66 by 5%   **d**   Increase 720 kg by 25%

   e   Increase £36 by 1%   **f**   Decrease 450p by 15%

2   Find these correct to 2 decimal places.

   a   Increase £56 by 12%   **b**   Decrease $49 by 22%

   c   Decrease 39 kg by 36%   **d**   Increase 230 g by 38%

   e   Increase €560 by 7%   **f**   Decrease 1340 m by 73%

   g   A computer costs £499 before VAT is added. VAT is 17.5%. Increase the cost of the computer by 17.5% to find the cost of the computer when the VAT is added.

   h   A holiday costs £2695 but it is reduced by 9% in a sale. Work out the cost of the holiday when it is in the sale.

3   Use an appropriate method to work out each of these problems. Give your answer to 2 decimal places where necessary.

   a   A holiday costs £495 but it is reduced by 15% in a sale. Calculate the new price of the holiday.

   b   Mr Holmes earns £456 a week. He has a pay increase of 3%. Work out how much he will earn after the pay increase.

   c   A plumber charges Teresa £4389 for new central heating. If the bill is paid within 7 days he reduces the bill by 5%. Teresa pays within 7 days. Work out how much she saves.

4   Fred pays income tax at 20%.

He is allowed to earn £10 000 before he pays any income tax. He earns £22 500 in one year.

Work out how much income tax he pays in that year.

5   Gemma invests £100 in a bank account.

Simple interest of 4% is added at the end of each year.

Work out how much money Gemma has at the end of

   a   the first year   **b**   three years.

         1060, 1237, 1302, 1934   **SEARCH**

1 Write each of these ratios in the form 1: n.

  a $3 : 12$ **b** $5 : 35$ **c** $16 : 480$

  d $65p : £4.55$ **e** $35 \text{ g} : 35 \text{ kg}$ **f** $0.18 : 5.76$

2 **a** To make mortar you mix sand and cement in the ratio $5 : 2$. How much sand should be mixed with 20 kg of cement?

  b In a school the ratio of boys to girls is $6 : 5$. If there are 1760 students in the school, how many are girls?

  c A scale on a map is $1 : 250\ 000$. If a distance on the map is 5 cm, what is the distance in real life (in metres)?

  d A model car has a scale of $3 : 40$. What is the length of the model car if the real life car measures 8 metres?

3 Solve each of these problems.

  a Divide £25 in the ratio $3 : 2$

  b Divide £120 in the ratio $1 : 5$

  c Divide 144 kg in the ratio $5 : 7$

  d Divide 240p in the ratio $7 : 3$

  e Divide 132p in the ratio $5 : 6$

4 Calculate these percentage increases or decreases without using a calculator.

You must show all of your working.

  a Increase £250 by 10%   **b** Decrease £400 by 25%

  c Decrease £60 by 17.5%   **d** Increase 60p by 1%

  e Increase €300 by 15%   **f** Decrease \$320 by 35%

  g Decrease 80p by 65%   **h** Increase \$120 by 99%

5 Ayesha put £564 in a new savings account.

Simple interest of 4% was added to the amount in her savings each year.

Calculate the total amount in Ayesha's savings account at the end of 2 years.

13.1   Factors and multiples

1   **a**   From the numbers in the oval, write the common factors of 36 and 48.

    b   From the numbers in the oval, write the common multiples of 6 and 9.

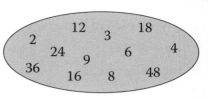

oval contents: 2   12   3   18   24   9   6   4   36   16   8   48

2   **a**   List all the factors of 36.

    b   List all the factors of 48.

    c   Find the highest common factor of 36 and 48.

3   Find the highest common factor of

    a   6 and 8   **b**   12 and 36   **c**   15 and 18

    d   72 and 48   **e**   81 and 27   **f**   28 and 24.

4   Find the lowest common multiple of

    a   3 and 4   **b**   7 and 6   **c**   9 and 5

    d   12 and 4   **e**   16 and 12   **f**   18 and 22.

5   **a**   Find the highest common factor (HCF) of 108 and 36.

    b   Find the highest common factor (HCF) of 72 and 96.

6   Find the

      i   HCF

      ii   LCM of these pairs of numbers.

    a   36 and 60

    b   45 and 120

    c   54 and 504

7   Isla beats her toy drum every 5 seconds. Ayesha blows a whistle every 12 seconds.

    If Isla and Ayesha begin at the same time, when do they next play their instruments together?

> Hint: Find the LCM of 5 and 12.
> Explain why this works.

Q 1032, 1034, 1044   **SEARCH**

Prime factor decomposition

1 Write down the numbers inside the oval that are

  a odd numbers

  b square numbers

  c cube numbers

  d factors of 18

  e prime factors of 36

  f highest common factor (HCF) of 24 and 18

  g lowest common multiple (LCM) of 6 and 4.

Numbers inside the oval: 2, 24, 144, 3, 24, 1, 36, 49, 6, 4, 16, 8, 5, 1000, 216, 100, 9

2 **a** Express 72 as a product of its prime factors.

  b Find the highest common factor (HCF) of 72 and 24.

3 1800 can be expressed by the product of prime factors

    $2^x \times 3^y \times 5^z$.

Find the values of x, y and z.

4 Use a factor tree to write each of these numbers as a product of its prime factors.

  a 60   **b** 210   **c** 378   **d** 504   **e** 2156

5 **a** Express 36 as the product of its prime factors.

  b Find the HCF of 36 and 90.

  c What is the LCM of 36 and 90?

6 Write each of these numbers as a product of its prime factors.

  a 210   **b** 540   **c** 1350

  d 1750   **e** 1694   **f** 4732

7 Find the LCM and HCF of these numbers.

  a 16, 24 and 32   **b** 10, 30 and 50

1   Use your calculator, where necessary, to work out these.

a 5^2 b 11^2 c 3^3

d 1^3 e $(-3)^2$ f 11^3

g $\sqrt{49}$ h $\sqrt{169}$ i $\sqrt[3]{27}$

j $\sqrt[3]{2197}$ k $\sqrt{2500}$ l $\sqrt[3]{1000}$

2   Use your calculator, where necessary, to work out each of these roots. Give your answer to a suitable degree of accuracy.

a $\sqrt{81}$ b $\sqrt{119}$ c $\sqrt[3]{8}$

d $\sqrt[3]{1728}$ e $\sqrt{784}$ f $\sqrt[3]{729}$

g $\sqrt{50}$ h $\sqrt[3]{120}$ i $\sqrt{12}$

j $\sqrt{250}$ k $\sqrt[3]{10\,000}$ l $\sqrt{101}$

3   Use your calculator to work out these questions. In each case copy the question and fill in the missing powers.

a $2^\square = 8$ b $3^\square = 27$ c $6^\square = 36$

d $5^\square = 125$ e $4^\square = 64$ f $10^\square = 1000$

g $2^\square = 32$ h $3^\square = 729$ i $2^\square = 1$

4   Work out the value of

a $(3^2)^3$ b $(\sqrt{4})^2$ c $a^2 \times a^4$

d $\dfrac{3^4 \times 3^5}{3}$ e 5^0

5   Some numbers can be represented as the sum of two squares.

For example, $4^2 + 5^2 = 16 + 25 = 41$.

Find all the numbers between 1 and 50 that can be represented as the sum of two square numbers.

1 Here is a list of numbers.

3, 4, 6, 8, 12, 18, 24, 30, 36, 48, 72

Write the numbers which are

a factors of 12

b multiples of 6

c factors of both 12 and 8

d multiples of both 6 and 8

e factors of 72

f highest factor of 72.

2 Find the HCF and LCM of each pair of numbers.

a 60 and 72　　　**b** 24 and 40　　　**c** 24 and 29

3 Find the HCF and LCM of each set of three numbers.

a 24, 36, 60　　　**b** 48, 72, 240　　　**c** 21, 63, 504

4 **a** Express 60 and 108 as products of their prime factors.

b Use your answer to part **a** to work out the HCF of 60 and 108.

5 Use your calculator, where necessary, to work out these powers and roots.

a 6^2 　　　　　**b** 14^2 　　　　　**c** 4^3

d 1^3 　　　　　**e** 15^2 　　　　　**f** $(-6)^2$

g 7^3 　　　　　**h** 12^3 　　　　　**i** 10^3

j $\sqrt{81}$ 　　　　**k** $\sqrt{169}$ 　　　　**l** $\sqrt[3]{64}$

m $\sqrt[3]{17\,576}$ 　　**n** $\sqrt{4900}$ 　　　**o** $\sqrt[3]{1000}$

6 Use your calculator to work out each of these

a 18^3 　　**b** 9^5 　　**c** 3^9 　　**d** 11^4 　　**e** 5^5

14.1 Drawing straight-line graphs

1 These coordinates lie on a straight line.
$(-2, 1) (-1, 2) (0, 3) (1, 4) (2, 5) (3, 6)$
Copy and complete these statements.
The y-value is always equal to ___ + the x-value.
The equation of the line is $y = $ ___ .

2 a Copy and complete this table of values for the equation $y = 2x - 2$.

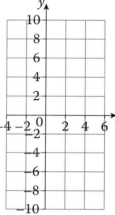

x	−4	−2	0	2	6
y	−10				

b Write a list of coordinate pairs from your table.
c Copy the grid and plot the points from part **b**.
Join them with a straight line.
d From your graph, find the value
of y when $x = 4$.

3 a Copy and complete the table of values for $y = -2x + 4$.

x	−2	−1	0	1	2
y					

b Write the coordinate pairs.
c Plot the line $y = -2x + 4$ onto a grid with appropriate axes.

4 Match the equations to the graphs of straight lines.

$y = -3$
$y = x - 3$
$x = -3$
$x = 2$
$y = 2$
$y = -3x - 2$
$y = 2x + 2$
$y = -\frac{1}{2}x + 2$ $y = -x - 3$

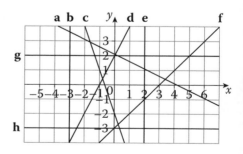

Hint: Beware, there are some extra equations!

5 Draw the graphs of these functions, each on a separate grid with axes from −10 to +10.
a $y = 2x + 4$ **b** $y = 5x - 4$ **c** $x + y = 5$ **d** $4x - y = 5$

 Q 1093, 1394, 1395, 1396   SEARCH

1 **a** Rearrange these equations into the form $y = mx + c$.

  i $2x + y = 6$ **ii** $3y - 6x = -9$

  iii $10y + 5x = 40$ **iv** $2y - 4x = -10$

 b Write the equation of the line parallel to line $y = 2x + 6$.

2 Write three equations of straight lines that are parallel to

 a $y = 4x - 5$ **b** $y = -5x - 5$.

3 Write the equations of these lines in order of steepness, starting with the least steep.

 a $y = 3x + 4$ **b** $2x - y = 10$

 c $y = 4x + 5$ **d** $6y - 3x = 12$

 e $4y + x = 20$ **f** $y = \dfrac{3}{4}x - 2$

 g $y - 10x = 5$ **h** $5x - 4y = 20$

4 Write

 i the coordinate of the y-intercept

 ii the gradient of each of these straight-line graphs.

 a $y = 3x + 4$ **b** $y = 5x - 1$

 c $y = 6 - 3x$ **d** $x + y = 2$ Hint: $y = ?$

 e $2y = 8 - x$ **f** $4x - 2y = 3$

5 Find the equation of a line that is parallel to $y = 4 - x$ and cuts the y-axis at $(0, 1)$.

6 Write the equations of these three lines.

 a Line A has a gradient of 3 and crosses the y-axis at $(0, 2)$.

 b Line B has a gradient of 4 and passes through $(1, -1)$.

 c Line C passes through $(0, 7)$ and $(3, -5)$.

14.3 Distance–time graphs

1 The distance–time graph shows Mick's bike ride to a local park.

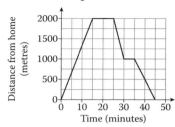

a How long did it take him to get there?

b How long did he spend at the park?

c What happened on the way home?

d For which part of the journey was Mick travelling the slowest? How can you tell?

2 The graph shows Teresa's journey to the shops.

a How many times did she stop on the way?

b Using the formula

$$\text{speed} = \frac{\text{distance}}{\text{time}}$$

work out the speed in metres per minute between

i 0 and 10 minutes

ii 20 and 60 minutes

iii 85 and 100 minutes.

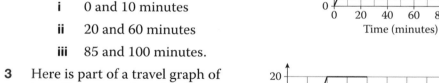

3 Here is part of a travel graph of David's journey from his house to the shops and back.

a Work out David's speed for the first 20 minutes of the journey.

David spent 10 minutes at the shops.

He then travelled back to his house at 80 km/h.

b Copy and complete the travel graph.

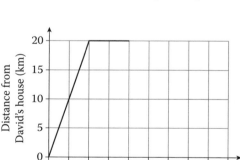

Hint: If speed = $\frac{\text{distance}}{\text{time}}$,

distance = speed × time,

and time = $\frac{\text{distance}}{\text{speed}}$.

Q 1322, 1323 SEARCH

1 **a** Copy and complete this table for the function $y = 2x + 4$.

x	0	1	2	3	4	5
y						

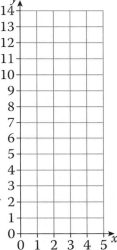

b On a copy of the grid, draw the graph
of $y = 2x + 4$.

c Draw the lines $y = 9$ and $x = 3$ on the same grid.

d Write the equation of a line that is
parallel to $y = 2x + 4$.

2 Write

i the coordinate of the y-intercept

ii the gradient of each of these straight-line graphs.

a $y = 3x + 4$ **b** $y = 5x - 1$

c $y = 6 - 3x$ **d** $x + y = 2$

e $2y = 8 - x$ **f** $4x - 2y = 3$

3 Anna goes for a run to the park. This distance–time
graph illustrates her journey.

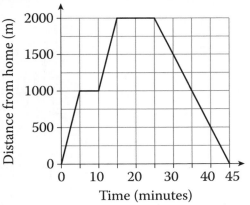

a How long does it take her to reach the park?

b How long does she stay at the park?

c When was she running the slowest?

d How far did she run in total?

15.1 3D shapes

1 Write the mathematical names for these 2D and 3D shapes.

a b c d e

f g h i j

2 Draw the nets for shapes **b**, **d**, **e**, **f** and **i** in question **1**.

3 a Draw the net for this cuboid.

   b Calculate the total area of the cuboid's faces.

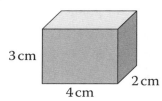

3 cm
2 cm
4 cm

4 On squared paper draw

   i the plan   ii the front elevation

   iii the side elevation of these solids.

a   b 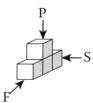 c   d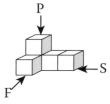

5 Here are the plan and front elevation of a prism.
   The front elevation shows the cross-section of the prism.

   a On squared paper draw a side elevation of the prism.

   b Draw a 3D sketch of the prism.

Plan

Front elevation

Q 1078, 1098, 1106   **SEARCH**

Volume of a prism

1 Using this formula work out the volume of the shapes.

Volume of prism = area of cross-section × length

a
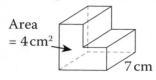
Area = 4 cm² → 7 cm

b
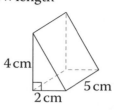
4 cm 2 cm 5 cm

c
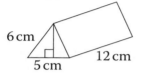
6 cm 5 cm 12 cm

d
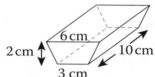
2 cm 6 cm 3 cm 10 cm

2 Work out the volume of this prism.

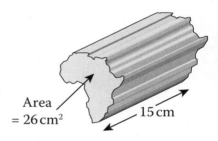
Area = 26 cm² 15 cm

3 Calculate the volume of each cuboid.
State the units in your answer.

a

5 cm 3 cm 6 cm

b

4.5 cm 3 cm 3.5 cm

c
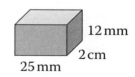
12 mm 2 cm 25 mm

4 A cylinder of height 15 cm is shown.
The diameter of the circle is 5 cm.

Calculate

a the area of the circle

b the volume of the cylinder.

5 cm 15 cm

Volume and surface area

1 Find the volume of each solid.

a

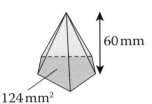
15 cm
5 cm
8 cm

b

60 mm
124 mm²

c

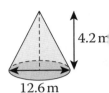
4.2 m
12.6 m

2 For all questions, give your answer to 3 significant figures.
Find the surface area of each solid.

a Regular tetrahedron of side 4 cm.

b Square-based pyramid, base length = 10 cm, vertical height above mid-point of square base = 12 cm.

3 Find the curved surface area of each cone.

a

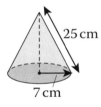
25 cm
7 cm

b

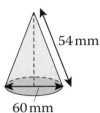
54 mm
60 mm

c

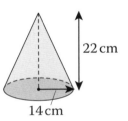
22 cm
14 cm

> Hint: Use the formula: Curved surface area of cone = πrl

4 Both of these
sectors are folded
to form cones.
Find the curved surface
area of each cone.

a

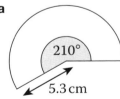
210°
5.3 cm

b

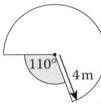
110°
4 m

5 For all questions, give your answers to 1 decimal place.
Find **i** the volume **ii** the surface area for each sphere.

a

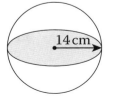
14 cm

b

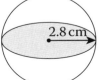
2.8 cm

c

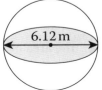
6.12 m

Q 1107, 1122, 1136 **SEARCH**

1 Draw a sketch of the nets for these shapes. Name the shapes.

a **b**

2 **a** Draw the nets of these cuboids.
 b Work out **i** the surface area
 ii the volume of each cuboid.

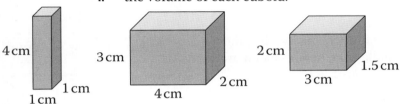

3 Find the surface area of these solids.

a 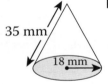 **b** **c** 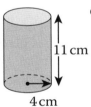 **d**

4 The diagram shows a solid cylinder with
a height of 12 cm and radius 5 cm.
Calculate the volume of the cylinder.
Give your answer correct to
3 significant figures.

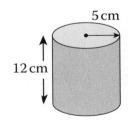

5 A sphere has a surface area of 100 cm^2.
Calculate the volume of the sphere.

> Hint: Find the radius of the sphere using the formula:
> surface area = $4\pi r^2$

Frequency diagrams

1 This frequency chart shows the heights of 30 children.

Copy and complete this frequency table for the information on the chart.

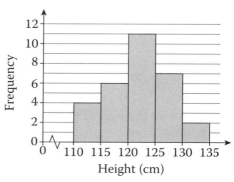

Height, h (cm)	Frequency
$110 < h \le 115$	

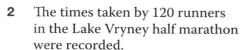

2 The times taken by 120 runners in the Lake Vryney half marathon were recorded.

Draw a histogram to illustrate this information.

Time, t (hours)	Frequency
$1 < t \le 1.25$	14
$1.25 < t \le 1.5$	26
$1.5 < t \le 1.75$	35
$1.75 < t \le 2$	24
$2 < t \le 2.25$	18
$2.25 < t \le 2.5$	3

3 The heights, in cm, of plants in a garden were recorded.

Draw a histogram to show the heights of the plants.

Height, h (cm)	Frequency
$5 < h \le 10$	6
$10 < h \le 15$	13
$15 < h \le 20$	16
$20 < h \le 25$	9
$25 < h \le 30$	4

4 The yield of tomatoes from plants in a greenhouse was recorded.

Yield of tomatoes	Number of plants
1–5	8
6–10	10
11–15	7
16–20	5

a How many plants were in the sample?

b Draw a bar chart to show the yield of tomatoes.

Q 1193, 1196   **SEARCH**

6.2 Averages and spread 2

1 Chris asked 50 people how much they paid for a new computer.
The results are shown in this frequency table.

Price, p (£)	Number of computers
$0 < p \leq 500$	2
$500 < p \leq 1000$	15
$1000 < p \leq 1500$	14
$1500 < p \leq 2000$	10
$2000 < p \leq 2500$	9

Calculate an estimate for the mean price paid for a new computer.

2 Some students took a mental
arithmetic test. Their marks are shown
in the frequency table.

Mark	Frequency
5	1
6	2
7	3
8	10
9	14
10	1

  a Work out how many students took
the test.

  b Write the modal mark.

25 students had a higher mark than
Sharon.

  c Work out Sharon's mark.

  d Find the median mark.

  e Work out the range of the marks.

3 A furniture company keeps a record of
its sales in one week. The table gives
information about those sales which
are £500 or less.

Cost, c (£)	Frequency
$0 < c \leq 100$	3
$100 < c \leq 200$	10
$200 < c \leq 300$	18
$300 < c \leq 400$	12
$400 < c \leq 500$	7

  a Calculate an estimate for the mean
from this table.

  b Find the class interval in which the
median lies.

  c There was only one other sale this
week, not included in the table.
This sale cost £1500.
The manager says, 'The class interval in which the
median lies will change.' Is the manager correct?
Explain your answer.

Scatter graphs and correlation

1   10 men took part in a long jump competition.
    The table shows the heights of the 10 men and the best
    jumps they made.

Height of men (m)	1.70	1.80	1.65	1.75	1.65	1.74	1.60	1.75	1.60	1.67
Best jump (m)	5.33	6.00	5.00	5.95	4.80	5.72	4.60	5.80	4.40	5.04

a   Plot the points on a scatter graph.

b   Describe in words the relationship between the height of the men
    and the maximum distance they jumped.

c   State the type of correlation shown in this graph.

2   The table shows the heights in m, and masses in kg, of 10 footballers.

Height	1.73	1.65	1.79	1.75	1.84	1.81	1.89	1.76	1.80	1.84
Mass	73	63	82	70	83	79	91	74	84	86

a   Draw a scatter graph to show these data on suitable axes.

b   State the type of correlation between height and weight of the
    football players.

c   Draw a line of best fit.

d   Use your line of best fit to estimate a footballer's
    i   height if their mass is 75 kg
    ii   mass if their height is 1.69 m.

3   The table shows the engine size and maximum speed of 10 cars.

Maximum speed (mph)	100	94	84	113	131	135	135	107	142	134
Engine size (cc)	1300	1100	1000	1600	2000	2700	2800	1400	2900	2500

a   Plot a scatter graph for these data on suitable axes.

b   Describe the relationship between the car's engine size and its
    maximum speed.

c   If a car's maximum speed is 115 mph, estimate its engine size to the
    nearest 100.

Q 1213, 1250   SEARCH

5.4 Time series

1 The number of text messages Sam sent over a week is given.

Day	Mon	Tue	Wed	Thur	Fri	Sat	Sun
Number of text messages	7	12	8	17	23	38	19

Draw a line graph to show this information.

2 The attendance, to the nearest 1000, at premiership football games in the 90s is shown.

Years	1992-3	1993-4	1994-5	1995-6	1996-7
Attendance	21 000	23 000	24 000	28 000	28 000

a Draw a line graph to show this information.

b Between which two years was there the biggest increase in attendance?

3 Stephen is on a diet and his mass in kg is recorded over 10 months. His mass each month is shown.

Month	Jan	Feb	Mar	Apr	May	Jun	Jul	Aug	Sep	Oct
Mass in kg	108	103	101	99	97	94	93	95	94	94

Draw a line graph to show his mass.

4 The following data show the brightness of the star *Delta Cephei* measured over a number of days.

Time (hours)	0	16	48	64	92	100	112
Brightness	4.32	4.19	3.95	3.85	3.61	3.65	3.85
Time (hours)	120	130	160	200	215	245	260
Brightness	4.10	4.30	4.05	3.75	3.60	3.98	4.29

a Plot this data on a graph.

b Comment on any patterns in the data.

1 Here is a record of the heights, in cm, of pea plants.

21 22 11 16 22 13 11 25 9 17 21 24 27
25 12 14 8 12 6 17 19 26 26 18 21 13
23 7 12 26 14 8 12 26 17 19 23 29 21

a Copy and complete the frequency table.

b How many pea plants were over 20 cm tall?

c What was the most common height for the pea plants?

Height, *h* (cm)	Tally	Frequenc
$5 < h \le 10$		
$10 < h \le 15$		
$15 < h \le 20$		
$20 < h \le 25$		
$25 < h \le 30$		

2 This table shows the time taken in minutes by a group of 40 Mathematics teachers to solve a Sudoku puzzle.

Time, *t*	$0 \le t < 5$	$5 \le t < 10$	$10 \le t < 15$	$15 \le t < 20$	$20 \le t < 25$
Frequency	2	6	12	7	3

Use this information to find
a the modal class **b** the class containing the median time
c an estimate of the mean time.

3 The table shows the number of units of electricity used in heating a house ten different days and the average temperature for each day.

Average temperature (°C)	6	2	0	6	3	5	10	8	9	12
Units of electricity used	28	38	41	34	31	31	22	25	23	22

a Plot the points on a scatter graph.
b Describe in words the relationship between the average temperature an the number of units of electricity used.
c State the type of correlation shown in this graph.

4 This table gives information about the length of 100 babies at birth.

Length, *l* (cm)	Frequency
$45 < l \le 48$	15
$48 < l \le 50$	22
$50 < l \le 51$	39
$51 < l \le 54$	18
$54 < l \le 56$	6

Draw a histogram to illustrate this information.

.1 **Calculating with roots and indices**

1 Calculate these using a calculator. Give your answers to
2 dp where appropriate.

   a $\sqrt{49}$ **b** $\sqrt{81}$ **c** $\sqrt{66}$

   d $\sqrt[3]{1000}$ **e** $\sqrt[3]{482}$ **f** $\sqrt[3]{1314}$

2 Use the x^y-button (or power key) on your calculator to solve these
equations. In each case, copy the equation and find the value of x.

   a $4^x = 16$ **b** $5^x = 125$ **c** $10^x = 1\,000\,000$

   d $x^4 = 4096$ **e** $2^x = 1024$ **f** $x^{10} = 1$

3 Find the value of these expressions.

   a $3^2 \times 4$ **b** $2^4 \times 5^2$ **c** $3 \times 5^3 \times 11$

   d $3^2 \times 5 \times 13$ **e** $2 \times 5^3 \times 3$ **f** $2 \times 11^2 \times 13$

   g 3×11^4 **h** $5^3 \times 11^2$ **i** $2 \times 3 \times 5 \times 13$

4 Simplify these expressions, giving your answers in index form.

   a $2^5 \times 2^3$ **b** $4^3 \times 4^6$ **c** $8^6 \times 8$

   d $x^2 \times x^7$ **e** $5^9 \div 5^4$ **f** $10^7 \div 10^6$

   g $a^8 \div a^8$ **h** $9^4 \div 9^7$ **i** $3^2 \times 3^2 \times 3^2$

   j $y^2 \times y^3 \times y^4$ **k** $6^5 \div 6^2 \times 6^4$ **l** $7^6 \times 7^4 \div 7^3$

5 Evaluate these expressions.

   a 10^0 **b** $(2^4)^2$ **c** $(\sqrt{5})^2$ **d** 2005^1

6 Write

   a 8 as a power of 2   **b** 64 as a power of 4

   c 81 as a power of 3   **d** 100 000 as a power of 10

   e 1296 as a power of 6   **f** $\frac{1}{4}$ as a power of $\frac{1}{2}$.

7 Use your calculator, where necessary, to evaluate these expressions.

   a 4^2 **b** 12^2 **c** 4^3

   d 2^3 **e** 17^2 **f** $(-2)^2$

   g $12^2 + 4^3$ **h** $13^2 - 4^3$ **i** $5^3 - 9^2$

   j $13^2 + 14^2 + 15^2$ **k** $3^3 + 4^3 + 5^3$ **l** $13^3 - 12^2 - 11$

8 Calculate each of these.

   a 1.4×10 **b** $4.5 \times 10\,000$ **c** $766 \div 10$

   d 4.5×10^3 **e** $54 \div 100$ **f** $23.9 \div 10^2$

   g 2.05×10^2 **h** $35.6 \div 10^3$ **i** 0.345×10^4

Exact calculations

1 Say whether each of these numbers is rational or irrational.

    a $\sqrt{49}$ **b** 7π **c** $\sqrt[3]{11}$

2 Calculate these, leaving π in your answers.

    a The area of a circle of diameter 14 cm.

    b The volume of a hemisphere of radius 6 m.

    c The radius of a circle of circumference 18 mm.

3 Find the exact values of the following fractions.

    a $\dfrac{2}{9} + \dfrac{1}{4}$ **b** $\dfrac{7}{12} - \dfrac{5}{8}$ **c** $\dfrac{8}{15} + \dfrac{5}{6}$

    d $\dfrac{5}{12} + \dfrac{7}{8} - \dfrac{2}{3}$ **e** $2\dfrac{2}{5} + 7\dfrac{1}{2}$ **f** $4\dfrac{3}{7} - 2\dfrac{2}{5}$

    g $\dfrac{4}{9}\left(\dfrac{3}{4} - \dfrac{7}{16}\right)$

4 Find the exact values of the following fractions.

    a $\dfrac{4}{5} \times \dfrac{11}{12}$ **b** $8\dfrac{1}{2} \times 2\dfrac{2}{3}$ **c** $\left(\dfrac{9}{20}\right)^2$

    d $\left(2\dfrac{1}{4}\right)^3$ **e** $3\dfrac{3}{4} \div 2\dfrac{1}{2}$ **f** $2\dfrac{2}{5} \div 7\dfrac{1}{10}$

5 **a** How many 75 cl bottles of lemonade can be filled from a 6 litre container?

    b $\dfrac{1}{4}$ of Ben's CD collection is jazz, $\dfrac{3}{5}$ is heavy metal and the rest is garage.

       What fraction of Ben's CD collection is garage?

6 Simplify the following expressions.

    a $\sqrt{3}(2\sqrt{3} + 4)$ **b** $\pi(7 - 3^2)$

    c $(5\sqrt{8})^3$ **d** $\pi\sqrt{5}\left(\sqrt{5} - \dfrac{1}{\sqrt{5}}\right)$

.3 Standard form

1 Write these numbers in standard form.

   a   600   **b**   19 340   **c**   2 000 000

   d   15   **e**   17 504   **f**   718 300

2 Write these numbers in standard form.

   a   0.16   **b**   0.005 32   **c**   0.060 01

   d   0.04   **e**   0.000 000 7   **f**   0.004 321

3 Convert these numbers in standard form to ordinary numbers.

   a 6.3×10^2 **b** 14.05×10^6 **c** 1.934×10^3

   d 7×10^5 **e** 8.3×10^0 **f** 16.4×10^1

4 Convert these numbers in standard form to ordinary numbers.

   a 4.8×10^{-2} **b** 6×10^{-5} **c** 2.003×10^{-3}

   d 2.9×10^{-1} **e** 8.999×10^{-8} **f** 1.717×10^{-10}

5 Work these out using a calculator, giving your answer in standard form.

   a $(2.4 \times 10^5) \times (1.92 \times 10^{-3})$ **b** $(4.7 \times 10^8) \div (3.2 \times 10^3)$

   c $(1.26 \times 10^{-3}) \div (2.52 \times 10^{-4})$ **d** $(6.39 \times 10^4) \div (3.6 \times 10^{-2})$

   e $(2.9 \times 10^6) \times (4.21 \times 10^{-2})$ **f** $(1.96 \times 10^{-3}) \times (5.2 \times 10^7)$

6 In astronomy, large distances are measured in a unit of length called the parsec.

One parsec is approximately 3.0857×10^{13} km.

Light travels at approximately 299 800 km/s.

One year has 31 536 000 seconds in it.

   a   **i**   Convert 299 800 into standard form.

         ii   Convert the number of seconds in a year into standard form.

   b   How many km does light travel in one year?
(This distance is called a light year.)

   c   How many light years are there in a parsec?

   d   The nearest star to our Solar System is called *Proxima Centauri*.
This star is approximately 1.3 light years from our Solar System.
Work out these distances, giving your answer in standard form.

         i   How many parsecs is *Proxima Centauri* from our Solar System?

         ii   How many km is *Proxima Centauri* from our Solar System?

1 Work out these, giving your answer as a power of 10.

a $10^4 \times 10^8$

b $10^{12} \div 10^7$

c $10^3 \div 10^9$

d $10^5 \times 10^4 \div 10^2$

e $10^8 \div 10^4 \times 10^{-3}$

f $10^5 \div 10^{-4} \times 10^6$

g $10^2 \times 10^2 \times 10^2 \times 10^2$

h $\dfrac{10^{-8} \times 10^3}{10^7 \times 10^{-9}}$

2 Find the value of x in these equations.

a $x^3 = 125$

b $x^2 = \dfrac{1}{16}$

c $1\dfrac{1}{4}x = 4\dfrac{3}{8}$

d $7^x = 49$

e $2^x = 512$

f $x^7 = 16\,384$

g $(3.5)^x = 42.875$

h $\sqrt[3]{x} = 7$

i $x^4 = 1$

j $4^x = 1$

3 a Sean travels $\dfrac{5}{7}$ of his journey to work by tram. He walks the remaining 390 m.

What is the length of his tram journey?

b Sean's tram travels at an average speed of 39 m/min, and his whole journey takes him exactly one hour. What is Sean's average walking speed?

c 4 goals are scored in a football match of 90 minutes. The time from the start of the match to the first goal, the intervals between the goals and the time from the last goal to the end of the match are all the same. In what minute was the third goal scored?

4 a Write these numbers in standard form.

i 500

ii 2140

iii 120 000

iv 895.3

b Write these numbers as ordinary numbers.

i 4.2×10^3

ii 5.02×10^5

iii 7×10^6

iv 5.125×10^2

5 Work these out without using a calculator, giving your answer in standard form.

a $(8 \times 10^4) \div (4 \times 10^2)$

b $(9.6 \times 10^{-8}) \div (3 \times 10^{-5})$

c $(6 \times 10^{-4}) \times (5 \times 10^9)$

d $(2.4 \times 10^3) \times (5 \times 10^4)$

e $(3 \times 10^5) \div (6 \times 10^{-2})$

Properties of quadratic functions

.1

1 Match these graphs to their equations.

a $y = 2x + 4$

b $y = x^2$

c $y = -3$

d $y = x^2 - 4$

e $y = -x + 3$

f $y = -2x + 3$

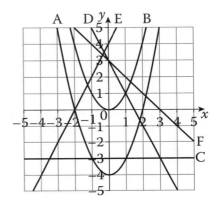

2 The point (2, 9) lies on which of these quadratic graphs?

$y = x^2 - 2x + 1$ $y = x^2 - 3x - 10$ $y = 2x^2 + 1$

$y = 3x^2 - 2x - 1$ $y = x^2 + 4x - 3$

3 a Copy and complete this table of values to generate coordinates for the graph of $y = x^2 + 2x$.

x	−3	−2	−1	0	1	2	3
x²		4					
2x		−4					
y		0					

b By drawing appropriate axes, plot the coordinates that you have found in part **a** and join them to form a smooth parabola.

c Write the coordinates of the minimum point of this parabola.

d Write the roots of the function.

4 Use algebra to find the roots of these functions.

a $x^2 + x - 6$ **b** $x^2 + 6x + 8$ **c** $x^2 + 2x - 15$

1 **a** Copy and complete this table of values to generate coordinates for the graph of the function $y = x^3 + 2x^2$.

x	−3	−2	−1	0	1	2
x³	−27					
2x²	18					
y	−9					

b Draw and label an x-axis from −3 to 2 and a y-axis from −10 to 20. Plot the coordinates from the table in part **a**.

c Write the coordinates of the turning points of this cubic graph.

> Hint: The turning points are literally the points where the graph turns a corner and changes direction. The gradient will change from positive to negative or negative to positive.

2 **a** Copy and complete the table of values for the graph of the function $y = \dfrac{6}{x}$ for $-6 \leq x \leq 6$.

x	−6	−5	−4	−3	−2	−1	0	1	2	3	4	5	6
y											1.5		

b Hence plot the graph of $y = \dfrac{6}{x}$.

c Use your graph to estimate the value of y when $x = 3.5$.

3 This is a sketch of the graph of the function $y = x^3 - x^2 - 6x$.

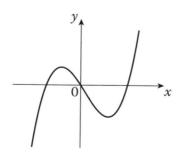

Find the roots of the function.

> Hint: Fully factorise $x^3 - x^2 - 6x$. Take out a factor of x to begin. Factorise the quadratic that remains.

Real-life graphs

1 The temperature $y\,°F$ is approximately related to the temperature $x\,°C$ by the formula

$$30 = y - 2x.$$

a Rearrange this formula into the form $y = mx + c$.

b Draw a graph of this formula on a grid from -20 to 40.

Use your graph to find

c **i** y when $x = 15°C$

ii y when $x = -10°C$

iii x when $y = 0°F$

iv x when $y = 100°F$

2 Plot a graph to represent the total cost of hiring a plumber if their call-out charge is £50 and they charge £20 an hour labour. The longest that they will take is 8 hours.

a Use your graph to work out the cost of hiring a plumber for 4 hours.

b How long did they spend on a job if the bill was £160?

c Write the equation of the line, stating the meaning of any letters used.

3 Here are three containers.

a **b** **c**

Water is poured into each container at a steady rate.

Match the correct graph of water height against time to fill its container.

i   ii   iii

1 **a** Copy and complete this table of values to generate coordinates for the graph of the function $y = x^2 - x - 6$.

x	−2	−1	0	0.5	1	2	3	4
x²	4							
−x	2							
−6	−6							
y	0			−6.25				

b By drawing appropriate axes, plot the coordinates that you have found in part **a** and join them to form a smooth parabola.

c Write the coordinates of the minimum point of this parabola.

d Find the roots of the function.

2 This is a conversion graph to convert British pounds to Australian dollars. Use the graph to convert

a **i** £50 to Australian dollars

ii AU$96 to pounds.

b If Julien has £60 and Alison has AU$120, who can purchase the most British goods if Alison converts her money?

c Write the equation of the line, stating the meaning of any letters used.

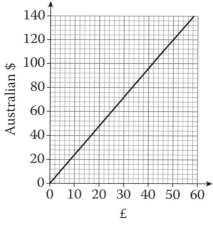

3 Sketch a graph to show the depth of water against time when these containers are filled.

a **b** **c** **d**

.1 Pythagoras' theorem

1 Calculate the length of the hypotenuse in these right-angled triangles. Give your answer to a suitable degree of accuracy.

a
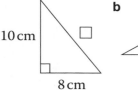
10 cm
8 cm

b
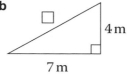
4 m
7 m

c
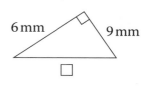
6 mm
9 mm

2 Calculate the lengths marked by letters in these right-angled triangles.

a
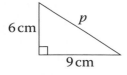
6 cm
p
9 cm

b
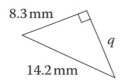
8.3 mm
q
14.2 mm

c
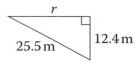
r
25.5 m
12.4 m

3 Calculate the perimeter and area of each shape.

a

14 cm
22 cm

b
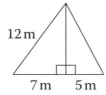
12 m
7 m   5 m

4 The diagram shows a cylinder of height 13 cm and a radius of 2.5 cm.
The length of a pencil is 14 cm.
Show that this pencil cannot fit inside the cylinder.
You cannot break the pencil.

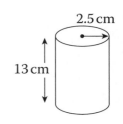
2.5 cm
13 cm

5 **a** Work out the length of the diagonal of a square of side 4 cm.

   b Work out the length of the diagonal of a rectangle with dimensions 7.5 cm and 3.5 cm.

19.2 Trigonometry 1

1 Use the tangent ratio to calculate the lengths marked by letters in these right-angled triangles.

a
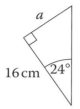
16 cm 24° a

b

9.3 mm 41° b

c
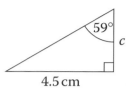
59° c 4.5 cm

2 Find the sides marked by letters in each of these right-angled triangles, giving your answers to 3 significant figures.

a
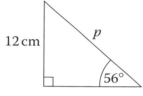
12 cm p 56°

b
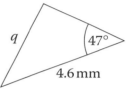
q 47° 4.6 mm

c
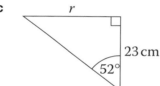
r 23 cm 52°

d
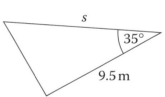
s 35° 9.5 m

3 Phil measures the angle of elevation from the ground where he is lying to the top of a cliff as 23°. He is exactly 60 m from the base of the cliff. By sketching a diagram and using trigonometry, work out the height of the cliff.

4 A rocky outcrop, *R*, is 55 km due west of a lighthouse, *L*, and due north of a ship, *S*. The lighthouse is on a bearing of 038° from the ship.

How far is the ship from the rocks, to the nearest km?

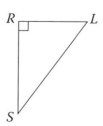
R L S

Trigonometry 2

1 Find the angles marked by letters in each of these right-angled triangles, giving your answers to 3 significant figures.

a
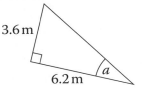
3.6 m
6.2 m
a

b
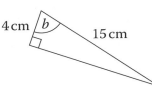
4 cm
b
15 cm

c
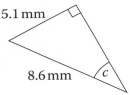
5.1 mm
8.6 mm
c

d
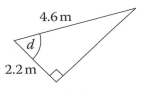
4.6 m
d
2.2 m

e
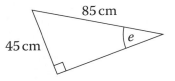
85 cm
45 cm
e

f
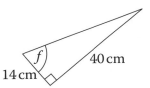
f
14 cm
40 cm

2 Find the sides marked by letters in each of these right-angled triangles, giving your answers to 3 significant figures.

a
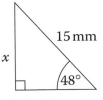
15 mm
x
48°

b
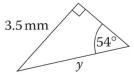
3.5 mm
54°
y

c
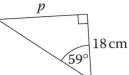
p
18 cm
59°

d
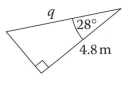
q
28°
4.8 m

e
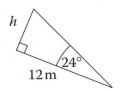
h
24°
12 m

f
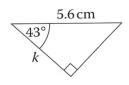
5.6 cm
43°
k

19.4 Vectors

1 Draw these vectors on square grid paper.

$$\mathbf{a} = \begin{pmatrix} -3 \\ 2 \end{pmatrix} \qquad \mathbf{b} = \begin{pmatrix} 6 \\ -4 \end{pmatrix} \qquad \mathbf{c} = \begin{pmatrix} -6 \\ -4 \end{pmatrix} \qquad \mathbf{d} = \begin{pmatrix} 2 \\ 3 \end{pmatrix}$$

   a Write a pair of vectors that are parallel.

   b Write a pair of vectors that are perpendicular.

2 *OABC* is a parallelogram.

$\overrightarrow{OA} = \mathbf{a}$ and $\overrightarrow{OC} = \mathbf{c}$

Find, in terms of **a** and **c**

   a $\overrightarrow{BC}$ **b** $\overrightarrow{AB}$ **c** $\overrightarrow{AC}$

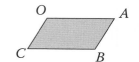

3 *OAB* is a triangle.

$\overrightarrow{OA} = \mathbf{a}$ and $\overrightarrow{OB} = \mathbf{b}$

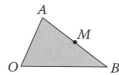

M is the midpoint of *AB*.
Find, in terms of **a** and **b**

   a $\overrightarrow{AB}$ **b** $\overrightarrow{BA}$ **c** $\overrightarrow{AM}$

4 *OPQR* is a trapezium.
PQ and *OR* are parallel.
PQ = 3*OR*

$\overrightarrow{OP} = \mathbf{p}$ and $\overrightarrow{OR} = \mathbf{r}$
Find, in terms of **p** and **r**

   a $\overrightarrow{PQ}$ **b** $\overrightarrow{OQ}$ **c** $\overrightarrow{QR}$

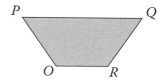

5 *OAB* is a triangle.
X is the midpoint of *OA*.
Y is the midpoint of *OB*.

$\overrightarrow{OA} = \mathbf{a}$ and $\overrightarrow{OB} = \mathbf{b}$
Find, in terms of **a** and **b**

   a $\overrightarrow{AB}$ **b** $\overrightarrow{OX}$ **c** $\overrightarrow{XY}$

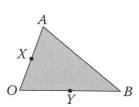

1 Calculate the unknown lengths in these right-angled triangles. Give your answers to a suitable degree of accuracy.

a
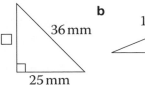
36 mm
25 mm

b
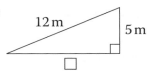
12 m
5 m

c
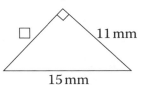
11 mm
15 mm

2 Find the sides marked by letters in each of these right-angled triangles, giving your answers to 3 significant figures.

a
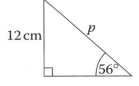
12 cm
p
56°

b
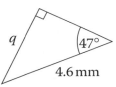
q
47°
4.6 mm

c
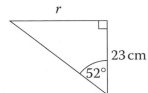
r
23 cm
52°

d
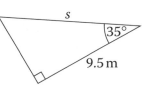
s
35°
9.5 m

3 *PQRS* is a triangle with *PS* = 12.2 cm, *QR* = 9.5 cm and angle *PQS* = 57°.

Find q.

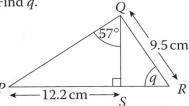
Q
57°
9.5 cm
P
12.2 cm
S
q
R

4 *OABC* is a trapezium. *OC* and *AB* are parallel.

$AB = \frac{2}{3} OC$

$\overrightarrow{OA} = \mathbf{a}$ and $\overrightarrow{OC} = \mathbf{c}$

Find, in terms of **a** and **c**

a $\overrightarrow{AB}$ **b** $\overrightarrow{OB}$ **c** $\overrightarrow{CB}$

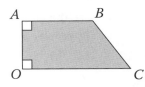
A
B
O
C

20.1   Sets

1   **a**   List the elements of these sets.

     i   S = the first 5 square numbers

     ii   M = the first 5 multiples of 4

     iii   F = the factors of 100

  b   Using the sets in part **a**, give the sets

     i $S \cap M$ **ii** $F \cup M$

     iii $S \cap M \cap F$ **iv** $(S \cup M \cup F)'$

2   Give, in words, a precise description of each set.

  a   {1, 3, 5, 7, 9}   **b**   {January, June, July}

  c   {23, 29, 31, 33, 37}   **d**   {1, 1, 2, 3, 5}

  e   {1, 2, 4, 5, 10, 20}

3   **a**   A survey of 100 air travellers found that 38 had flown with Cyanair and 27 with Flyme. Five had flown with both airlines.

     i   Draw a Venn diagram to show this information.

     ii   How many travellers had flown with neither airline?

     iii   How many travellers had flown with only one airline?

  b   The table shows where those 100 travellers last flew.

	Canada (C)		Canary Islands (S)		Capetown (SA)	
	Male	Female	Male	Female	Male	Female
Number	18	14	22	28	9	9

Use the information in the table to complete these Venn diagrams.

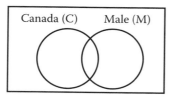

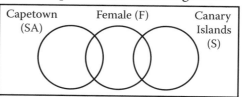

  c   Use the table and your Venn diagrams to write down the numbers in these sets.

     i $M \cap C$ **ii** $C \cap F$ **iii** $C \cap SA$ **iv** $SA \cap M$

     v $C \cup F$ **vi** $F \cap SA$ **vii** $S \cup M$

Q 1262, 1921, 1922   **SEARCH**

4 **a** Draw a Venn diagram to illustrate these sets.

    i ζ = {whole numbers from 1 to 21}   **ii**   F = {factors of 40}

    iii   T = {first 6 triangular numbers}

  b Using the Venn diagram in part **a**, give the sets

    i $T \cap F$ **ii** $T \cup F$ **iii** $(T \cup F)'$

  c The number of elements in a set, A, may be written as $n(A)$.

    Using the Venn diagram in part **a**, give the value of

    i $n(T \cap F)$ **ii** $n(T \cup F)$ **iii** $n(T \cup F)'$

1   Robert rolls a fair dice and spins a fair spinner.
One possible outcome is (6, blue).

a   Copy and complete the sample space diagram to show all
possible outcomes.

		Dice					
		1	2	3	4	5	6
Spinner	**Blue**						6, blue
	Red						
	Green						
	Yellow						

b   Find the probability of getting

i   a 6 and a blue
ii   a prime number and a red
iii a factor of 12 and a yellow
iv   a square number with any colour.

2   Laura's journey to work takes her through two
sets of traffic lights. When she arrives at each
set of lights they are both equally likely to be
showing red, amber or green.

		Second lights		
		R	A	G
First lights	**R**		RA	
	A			
	G			

a   Copy and complete this table
to show all nine possible
outcomes.

b   Copy and complete this
tree diagram to show all
nine possible outcomes.

c   Calculate the probability of
finding both sets of lights on
i   red
ii   different colours
iii the same colour.

d   Laura travels to work 180
times in a year. How often
can she expect both sets of
lights to be on red?

First
lights

Second
lights

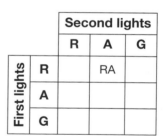

Q 1199, 1263   **SEARCH**

1   Daisy carries out a statistical experiment. She throws a coin 500 times. She throws a head 400 times.

     a   Is the coin fair? Explain your answer.

Daisy then throws two fair coins once.

     b   Copy and complete the probability tree diagram to show the possible outcomes.

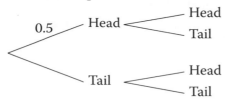

     c   Find the probability of throwing a head and a tail in any order on this throw of Daisy's fair coins.

2   A bag contains 5 aquamarine, 3 amethyst and 2 topaz gemstones. Rose throws a fair coin and selects a gemstone from the bag at random. Find the probability of selecting

     a   a head and an aquamarine gemstone

     b   a tail and a topaz gemstone.

     c   What can you say about the events 'select an amethyst' and 'throw a head'? Explain your answer.

3   A teacher requires two classroom monitors to be in charge of the register and collecting in work. She chooses two students at random from a class of 25 students: 15 boys and 10 girls.

     a   Draw a tree diagram to show all possible outcomes.

     b   Find the probability that the two students chosen are both boys.

> Hint: Choosing two students is the same as choosing without replacement. Remember to reflect this in the fractions that you use.

1   In a local road the residents can access television using a combination of broadband (B), cable (C), or a satellite dish (S).

26 homes can watch using broadband, 34 can watch using cable, and 21 can watch using a satellite dish. 8 homes can watch using either broadband or cable, and 3 homes can watch using either a satellite dish or cable. No homes can watch using either broadband or a satellite dish.

5 properties do not possess a television set.

a   Draw a Venn diagram with 3 intersecting circles, labelled B, C and S.

b   How many homes are there in the road?

c   Find the value of

i $n(B \cap S \cap C)$	**ii** $n(B \cup S \cup C)$	**iii** $n(B \cap S)$
iv $n(B \cap C)$	**v** $n(S \cap C)$	**vi** $n(B \cup S)$
vii $n(B \cup C)$	**viii** $n(S \cup C)$	**ix** $n(B \cup S \cup C)'$
x $n(B)'$	**xi** $n(B \cap S \cap C)'$	**xii** $n(S \cup C)'$

d   Find these probabilities.

i $P(B \cap S \cap C)$	**ii** $P(B \cup S \cup C)$	**iii** $P(B \cap S)$
iv $P(B \cap C)$	**v** $P(S \cap C)$	**vi** $P(B \cup S)$
vii $P(B \cup C)$	**viii** $P(S \cup C)$	**ix** $P(B \cup S \cup C)'$
x $P(B)'$	**xi** $P(B \cap S \cap C)'$	

2   A spinner has equally sized sections numbered 1 to 8. Alasdair spins the spinner and throws a fair coin.

a   Draw a table to show all possible outcomes.

b   Find the probability of obtaining

i   the number 2 and a head

ii   a number greater than 5 and a tail

iii an even number and a tail

iv   a prime number and a head.

3 Bag A contains 7 white marbles and 3 black marbles.
Bag B contains 2 white marbles and 4 red marbles.
Amelia chooses a marble at random from each bag.

   a Draw a tree diagram to show all possible outcomes.

   b Find the probability that the two marbles chosen are different colours.

   c Find the probability that at least one of the marbles chosen is red.

4 Jason and Clare play two games of tennis.
The probability that Jason will win any game against Clare is 0.55. Work out the probability that Jason wins at least one game.

21.1 Sequence rules

1 Find the next three terms in each sequence.
Give the rule that you used.

a 4, 7, 10, 13, ...   **b** 12, 15, 18, 21, 24, ...

c 1, 1.5, 2, 2.5, 3, ...   **d** 20, 17, 14, 11, ...

e 0.1, 0.2, 0.3, 0.4, 0.5, ... **f** −7, −3, 1, ...

2 Find the first five terms of these sequences.

a 1st term 4, increases by 5 each time

b 3rd term 5, decreases by 3 each time

c 2nd term 8, increases by 2 each time

d 3rd term −1, increases by 4 each time

e 2nd term 0, decreases by 3 each time

f 5th term 6, increases by 3 each time

3 For each of these sequences

i find the three missing terms

ii describe the sequence.

a 4, 7, □, 13, 16, □, 22, □

b 20, □, 12, 8, 4, □, □

c 7, 5, □, 1, □, □

d □, 10, 8, □, □, 2

e □, −15, −11, □, □, 1

f □, 15, □, 3, □

4 Find the first 3 terms and the 10th term of the sequences with these
position-to-term rules.

a $T(n) = 4n + 4$ **b** $T(n) = 5n + 2$ **c** $T(n) = 6n − 4$

d $T(n) = 3n + 5$ **e** $T(n) = 10n + 3$ **f** $T(n) = 10 − 2n$

5 Find the first 5 terms of the sequences with these position-to-term rules.

a $T(n) = n^2 + 3$ **b** $T(n) = n^2 − 3$ **c** $T(n) = 2n^2 + 3$

d $T(n) = 3n^2 − 4$ **e** $T(n) = 10 − n^2$ **f** $T(n) = 4n^2 − 5$

Finding the *n*th term

1   Here is a sequence.

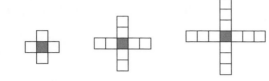

a   Write down the number of grey squares and white squares for the next two patterns.

b   Complete the table for the number of white squares.

Pattern number	1	2	3	4	5
Number of white squares			8		

c   Copy and complete this rule for the white squares.
Number of white squares = □ × pattern number.

d   Use your answers to parts **a** and **c** to write a rule for the total number of squares.

e   Use your rule from part **d** to work out the total number of squares in pattern number 10.

2   Repeat question **1** using this sequence of triangles instead of squares.

How many triangles will there be in the 10th pattern?

3   Find the *n*th term of these sequences.

a   12, 14, 16, 18, 20, ...   **b**   7, 12, 17, 22, 27, ...

c   10, 19, 28, 37, 46, ...   **d**   25, 22, 19, 16, 13, 10, ...

e   −3, −1, 1, 3, 5, 7, ...   **f**   −6, −9, −12, −15, −18, −21, ...

4   Given the following terms in a sequence,

15th term = 117

16th term = 125

17th term = 133

find an expression for the *n*th term of the sequence.

1 **a** What is the first cube number above 1 to also be a square number?

b What is the first triangular number above 1 to also be a square number?

2 Look at this number pattern.

$$1^2 = 1$$
$$2^2 = 1 + 3$$
$$3^2 = 1 + 3 + 5$$
$$4^2 = 1 + 3 + 5 + 7$$

a Write the next three lines in this pattern.

b Work out the value of k if

$50^2 = 1 + 3 + 5 + ... + k$.

3 Describe the following sequences using one of these words.

> arithmetic geometric
> quadratic Fibonacci-type

a 4, 7, 10, 13, ...   **b** 2, 4, 8, 16, ...

c 4, 8, 12, 20, 32, ...   **d** 3, 7, 15, 27, ...

e 4, −12, 36, −108, ...   **f** −4, −7, −11, −14, ...

g −16, −13, −8, −1, ...   **h** −3, −6, −9, −15, ...

4 Choose one of these nth terms for each of these sequences.

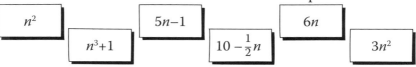

n^2 $5n-1$ $6n$

n^3+1 $10 - \frac{1}{2}n$ $3n^2$

a $9\frac{1}{2}, 9, 8\frac{1}{2}, 8, 7\frac{1}{2}, ...$ **b** 2, 9, 28, 65, 126, ...

c 6, 12, 18, 24, 36, ...   **d** 1, 4, 9, 16, 25, ...

e 4, 9, 14, 19, 24, ...   **f** 3, 12, 27, 48, 75, ...

5 Generate the first five terms of each of these sequences and comment on the behaviour of each.

a $T(n) = 5n - 3$ **b** $T(n) = n(n + 1)$ **c** $T(n) = 1 + \frac{1}{n}$

d $T(n) = n^2 + 5n + 4$ **e** $T(n) = (-2)^{n-1}$

> Hint: Use the words diverge, converge, limit and oscillate.

   🔍 1053, 1054, 1920, 1946   **SEARCH**

1 Find the next two terms in each of these number patterns.

    a   4, 8, 12, 16, 20, ...   **b**   3, 7, 11, 15, 19, ...

    c   100, 94, 88, 82, 76, ...   **d**   9, 16, 25, 36, 49, ...

    e   2, 4, 8, 16, 32, ...   **f**   1000, 500, 250, 125, 62.5, ...

    g   1, 1, 2, 3, 5, 8, ...   **h**   1, 2, 6, 24, 120, ...

2 Find the first five terms of the sequence with these position-to-term rules.

    a $T(n) = 3n + 1$ **b** $T(n) = 5n + 3$ **c** $T(n) = n^2 + 5$

    d $T(n) = 4n - 2$ **e** $T(n) = 9 - 3n$ **f** $T(n) = 2n^2 - 4$

3 Here is a pattern of hexagons.

    a   Copy and complete the table.

Pattern number	1	2	3	4	5	n
Term						

    b   Use the general formula to work out how many hexagons are needed for the 50th pattern.

4 Find the *n*th term of these linear sequences.

    a   7, 9, 11, 13, 15, ...   **b**   3, 6, 9, 12, 15, ...   **c**   3, 8, 13, 18, 23, ...

    d   −8, −4, 0, 4, 8, ...   **e**   17, 16, 15, 14, 13, ... **f**   20, 17, 14, 11, 8, ...

    g $1\frac{1}{2}, 2, 2\frac{1}{2}, 3, 3\frac{1}{2}, ...$ **h** $4\frac{3}{4}, 4\frac{1}{2}, 4\frac{1}{4}, 4, 3\frac{3}{4}, ...$

5 Look at this number pattern.

$$9^2 = 81$$
$$99^2 = 9801$$
$$999^2 = 998\ 001$$
$$9999^2 = 99\ 980\ 001$$

    a   Write the next two lines in this pattern. Use your calculator to check your answers.

    b   By relating the number of digits that are 9 in the question to the number of digits that are 9 in the answer, work out $99\ 999\ 999^2$.

Compound units

1 Copy and complete the table showing four journeys.

Person	Distance travelled	Time taken	Speed
Mrs Tomes	240 miles	3.2 hours	
Ms Howard	420 km	$3\frac{1}{4}$ hours	
Mrs Flynn	38 miles	20 minutes	
Mr Collins	10 km	12 minutes	

2 Caroline sets off from home for work at 7:45 a.m. and arrives at 8:10 a.m. She drives at an average speed of 56 km/h.

How far does Caroline travel to work?

3 A solid iron bar is in the shape of a cuboid of width 2 cm, height 12 cm and length 30 cm.

Iron has a density of $7.87\,g/cm^3$.

Work out the mass of the iron bar in kg to 3 significant figures.

4 The population of Sweden is approximately 9×10^6 people.

Sweden has an area of approximately $450\,000\,km^2$.

Work out the population density without using a calculator and giving your answer in standard form.

5 Karl receives 84 euros in exchange for £60.

a Calculate the rate of exchange in euros per £.

b How many euros would Karl get for £75?

c Karl's friend Ian receives 126 euros at the same rate of exchange. How many pounds did Ian exchange?

6 Melissa earns £8.70 per hour for 40 hours each week and 'time-and-a-half' if she works more than 40 hours. Melissa gets paid 'double time' if she works on Sundays. Calculate Melissa's pay if she works 45 hours from Monday to Friday and 8 hours on Sunday.

Direct proportion

1 A building contractor pays nine workers £1395 for
one day's work. How much would he pay

    a   5 workers   **b**   10 workers   **c**   15 workers?

2 If a 1.5 m length of copper piping has a mass of 9.9 kg,
work out the mass of these lengths of the same copper piping.

    a   0.5 m   **b**   3 m   **c**   5 m   **d**   12 m

3 A health food shop sells five different types of dried fruit.
Calculate the cost of 100 g of each type, given that

    a   200 g of apricots cost £2.20

    b   600 g of figs cost £3.60

    c   350 g of blueberries cost £4.90

    d   2 kg of raisins cost £8.00

    e   125 g of cranberries cost £2.00.

4 Fabric conditioner is sold in two differently sized bottles.
A standard bottle has a capacity of 750 ml and costs £1.26.
A large bottle has a capacity of 1.25 litres and costs £1.99.

Which bottle is the better value for money? Show your working.

5 The cost, C, of carpeting a room is directly proportional
to the area, a, of that room.

    a   Given that the cost of 7.5 m² of carpet for Rebecca's
bedroom is £168.75, find a formula connecting C and a.

    b   Use your formula to find the cost of carpeting the lounge,
which has an area of 14.5 m², in the same carpet.

    c   The dining room costs £236.25 to cover in the same
carpet. What is the area of the dining room?

22.3 Inverse proportion

1 The variable y is inversely proportional to the variable x.
Write the effect on y if x is

   a multiplied by 3   **b** divided by 6

   c multiplied by 0.75   **d** divided by 0.4.

2 An animal shelter has enough food to supply 12 dogs for 4 weeks
and 10 cats for 5 weeks.

   a How long would the dog food last for 8 dogs?

   b How long would the cat food last for 15 cats?

3 The number of people, n, required to build a wall is inversely
proportional to the time taken, t.

   a Given that it takes 10 people 4 hours to build this wall,
      find a formula connecting t and n.

   b How long would it take 8 people to build this wall?

   c How many people are required to build the wall in just
      20 minutes?

4 It takes 15 hours for 4 mechanics to service 16 bikes.

   a How many mechanics are needed to service 20 bikes in 15 hours?

   b How many hours will it take 4 mechanics to service 20 bikes?

   c How many mechanics are needed to service 16 bikes in 10 hours?

5 x is inversely proportional to y with $y = \dfrac{24}{x}$.

   a Create a table of values for x and y.

   b Plot each pair of coordinates and join the points with a smooth
      curve.

   c What is the product of the x- and y-coordinate for any point
      on the graph?

Q 1949   SEARCH

Growth and decay

1   Find the multiplier that gives the amount after each change.
     Write your answers as decimals.

    a   Increase of 50%   **b**   Decrease of 50%

    c   Increase of 5%   **d**   Decrease of 5%

    e   Increase of 0.5%   **f**   Decrease of 0.5%

2   The value of a house is £180 000. The value increases by 5% each year.

    a   Find a formula for the value of the house after *n* years.

    b   Use your formula to find the value of the house after 5 years.

3   Zac bought a van for £15 000.
     Each year the van decreased in value by 5%.
     Work out the value of Zac's van 2 years after he purchased it.

4   A bank pays compound interest of 4%. Find the amount of money in
     an account after 3 years if the original investment is £5000.

5   Mac wants to invest £500 for 5 years. His bank offers him two options.

       Option 1 is simple interest of 4.25% per annum.

       Option 2 is compound interest of 4% per annum.

   Which option should Mac choose in order to achieve
     the most interest on his investment? Show your working.

6   Philip's van decreases in value by 8% each year.
     After four years the van is worth £9170.

    a   What was the original cost of the van?

    b   What was the overall percentage depreciation of the
     van after 4 years?

    c   If the van continues to decrease in value at the same rate,
     after how many years will the van be worth less
     than £5000?

7   In 2011, the United Kingdom had a population of 62.2 million.
     If the population of the United Kingdom is increasing at,
     on average, an annual rate of 0.6%, calculate an estimate
     for the population of the United Kingdom in 2015.
     Give your answer to 3 significant figures.

1 The exchange rate for euros to pounds is approximately
£1 = €1.40.

Calculate how many euros you would get for

a £10 **b** £15 **c** £120 **d** £500.

Calculate how many pounds you would get for

e €5.60 **f** €154 **g** €168 **h** €224.

2 The area of the square is twice the area of the triangle.

Work out the **perimeter** of the square.

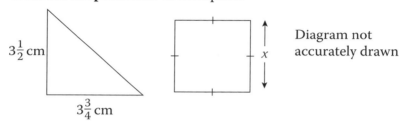

$3\frac{1}{2}$ cm

$3\frac{3}{4}$ cm

x

Diagram not accurately drawn

3 800 g of cornflakes cost £2.40. How much do 500 g of cornflakes cost?

4 Blank DVDs are sold in two different packs.

A pack of 4 DVDs costs £4.99.

A pack of 5 DVDs costs £6.19.

Which is the better buy?

5 y is inversely proportional to x. If $y = 20$ when $x = 16$, find

a a formula for y in terms of x

b the value of y when $x = 10$

c the value of x when $y = 15$.

6 Jake has £3500 in a bank account that earns 4.5% compound interest. Rowan has £3500 in a bank account that earns 4.7% simple interest. After 3 years, who will have the most money in their account assuming that no withdrawals have been made?

Revision homework

1 Write these numbers in words.

   a   67 000   **b**   40 007   **c**   687 900

   d   11 000 000   **e**   4 600 007   **f**   699 999

2 Work out these, giving your answer in its simplest form.

   a $\dfrac{1}{4} + \dfrac{5}{8}$ **b** $\dfrac{5}{7} - \dfrac{2}{5}$ **c** $3\dfrac{2}{7} - \dfrac{5}{8}$ **d** $\dfrac{23}{16} - \dfrac{-8}{15}$

   e $\dfrac{4}{9} \times \dfrac{3}{4}$ **f** $2\dfrac{1}{2} \div \dfrac{5}{9}$ **g** $4\dfrac{1}{9} \times 1\dfrac{13}{27}$ **h** $4\dfrac{2}{3} \div \dfrac{7}{8}$

3 Solve these equations.

   a $3x = 15$ **b** $2x + 4 = -4$ **c** $\dfrac{x}{3} + 3 = 6$

4 Calculate the area of these shapes. State the units.

   a 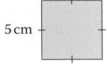   **b**

   c 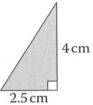   **d**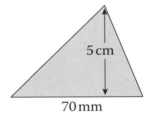

> Hint: units!

5 Round each of these numbers to the nearest

   i   2 sf   **ii**   3 sf

   a   5.269   **b**   26.392   **c**   0.3994   **d**   0.006 116

6 Calculate the size of the angles marked by letters.

   a 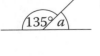   **b**   **c**   **d**

2   # Revision homework

1   For each of these give a suitable estimate.
       Show your workings clearly.

    a 9.74×4.98 **b** $92.7 \div 6.12$ **c** $\dfrac{12.94 \times 9.94}{5.87}$ **d** $\dfrac{78.9 \times 29.99}{25.4}$

2   The heights, in m, of 18 students in a class are recorded.

    1.67   1.72   1.80   1.59   1.60   1.64   1.74   1.81   1.52

    1.56   1.73   1.83   1.89   1.76   1.65   1.69   1.76   1.77

    a   Copy and complete an ordered stem-and-leaf diagram.

    15 | Key: 16 | 7 means 1.67 m
    16 |
    17 |
    18 |

    b   Calculate the **i**   mean   **ii**   mode   **iii**   median   **iv**   range.

3   Expand these expressions.

    a $x(3x + 2)$ **b** $x(x^2 + 3)$ **c** $3x(x^2 - 3)$ **d** $3x(x + 2)$
    e $2x(x^2 - 3)$ **f** $4x^2(x^2 + 2)$ **g** $5x(x^3 + 2)$ **h** $4x(x^2 + 3)$
    i $2x^2(x - 4)$ **j** $4x^2(x + 5)$

4   On square grid paper, draw the axes shown.

    a   Plot and join the points $(2, 1)$, $(4, 1)$, $(5, 4)$, $(3, 4)$.
       Label it shape A. Name the shape.

    b   Translate shape A by

    i $\begin{pmatrix} -5 \\ 1 \end{pmatrix}$ and label it B

    ii $\begin{pmatrix} -4 \\ -5 \end{pmatrix}$ and label it C

    iii $\begin{pmatrix} 1 \\ -4 \end{pmatrix}$ and label it D.

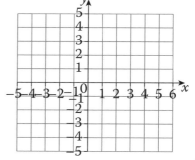

5   Calculate the
    i   circumference   **ii**   area of each circle

    a   **b**   **c**

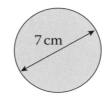

3 | Revision homework

1 Give the angle and direction of a rotation that is identical to a rotation of
   a 90° anticlockwise   **b** 150° clockwise
   c 335° clockwise   **d** 45° anticlockwise.

2 A 500 ml smoothie drink is made up of these juices

   33% strawberry   21% banana   22% orange
   11% grape   13% apple

   Calculate the number of ml of each type of juice.

3 Solve these equations.
   a $6b + 4 = 22$ **b** $5f - 4 = 26$ **c** $7f + 2 = 23$
   d $\frac{p}{4} + 3 = 12$ **e** $9m - 12 = 42$ **f** $\frac{r}{8} - 5 = -1$
   g $6d + 9 = 63$ **h** $r - 12 = -2$ **i** $6k + 4 = 19$
   j $3t + 5 = -13$ **k** $\frac{f}{6} - 6 = -1$ **l** $7p + 11 = -66$

4 Write these in order of size from lowest to highest.
   a $\frac{3}{5}$, 65%, $\frac{7}{8}$, 0.7   **b** 0.45, 49%, $\frac{4}{9}$, $\frac{4}{10}$
   c 33%, $\frac{1}{3}$, 25%, 0.3   **d** 99%, 1, $\frac{9}{10}$, 0.999
   e $\frac{4}{13}$, 25%, 0.09, $\frac{1}{5}$ **f** 0.15, 13%, $\frac{1}{13}$, $\frac{2}{23}$

5 180 people were asked what was their favourite sport. The results are shown in the table.
   a Calculate the number of people who liked other sports.
   b Calculate the angle one person represents in a pie chart.
   c Calculate the angle of each category in the pie chart.
   d Draw the pie chart.

Sport	Frequency
Football	64
Cricket	31
Rugby	28
Golf	29
Tennis	15
Other	

6 Calculate the third angle of each of these triangles and state the type of triangle.
   a 35°, 100°   **b** 45°, 90°   **c** 15°, 120°
   d 60°, 60°   **e** 27°, 143°   **f** 75°, 30°

4   Revision homework

1 Substitute the values $a = 2$, $b = 3$, $c = \dfrac{1}{2}$ into each expression.

    a $4a + b$ **b** $ac + 1$ **c** $2b - a$ **d** $6b + c$

    e $2a + b + 5c$ **f** $3c + 2a - b$ **g** $(a + b)^2$ **h** $2a^2 - 2c$

    i $\dfrac{bc}{a}$ **j** $3ab + 2bc$

2 Find the value of the angles marked by letters.

    a 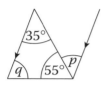   **b** 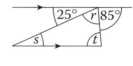   **c**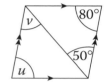

3   **a**   Simplify

         i $4g + 6g$ **ii** $3t \times 6p$

    b   Expand $6(3y - 4)$

    c   Expand and simplify $3(3p + 5) - 3(5p - 6)$

4 Calculate these, leaving your answers as fractions in their simplest form where necessary.

    a   What is the total weight of 9 shopping bags each weighing 2.5 kg?

    b   Elaine takes $\dfrac{3}{5}$ of an hour to run 5 miles. How long does it take her to run 12.5 miles?

    c   A rectangle is $\dfrac{2}{5}$ m long and $\dfrac{4}{7}$ m wide. What is the area of the rectangle? What is the perimeter of the rectangle?

5 A spinner is numbered 1 to 5.

    Dale spins the spinner and throws a coin.

    a   List all the possible outcomes.

    The spinner is biased.

Number	1	2	3	4	5
Probability	0.34	0.2	0.1	0.25	

    b   Work out the probability that the spinner will land on

         i   5   **ii**   6.

    c   Work out the probability that the spinner will land on an even number.

Revision homework

1 The area of this square is 4 times the area of the triangle.
Work out the **perimeter** of the square.

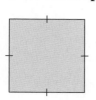 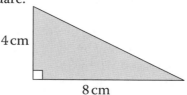

4 cm

Diagrams not
accurately drawn

8 cm

2 Expand and simplify these expressions.
a $5(6 + x)$ **b** $3(x + 4) + x$
c $3(3x - 6) + 5x$ **d** $7(3x + 2) + 6x + 2$
e $7x(x^2 - 6)$ **f** $5x(x + 2)$
g $4x(x^2 - 2)$ **h** $6x^2(x^2 + 5)$
i $5(x + 3) + 7(x - 2)$ **j** $5(2x + 6) + 6(x - 3)$
k $3(5x + 6) - 6(x + 3)$ **l** $3(5x - 2) - 3(x + 3)$

3 Convert these areas to the given units.
a $6 \text{ cm}^2 = $ ___ mm^2 **b** $900 \text{ mm}^2 = $ ___ cm^2
c $60\,000 \text{ mm}^2 = $ ___ m^2 **d** $10 \text{ m}^2 = $ ___ cm^2
e $9\,000\,000 \text{ m}^2 = $ ___ km^2 **f** $6 \text{ km}^2 = $ ___ m^2

4 The diagram shows part of a pattern. It is made
up of a regular pentagon, squares and an isosceles
triangle.
a Write the size of the angle marked x.
b Work out the size of the angle marked y.

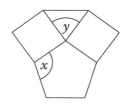

5 a Copy the diagram of a garden *ABCD*
using a scale of 1 cm to 1 m.
b Kevin places a sprinkler at point *A*.
The sprinkler waters the garden up to
5 m away as it rotates.
Kevin places a second sprinkler at point *C*.
It has a maximum reach of 4 m. Shade the
area of the garden that remains unwatered.

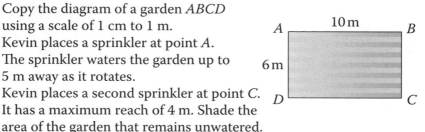

A   10 m   *B*

6 m

D   *C*

6 Solve this pair of simultaneous equations graphically.
$x - y = 2$
$y = 3x - 4$

6   Revision homework

1   Calculate these giving your answers correct to 2 decimal places.

    a   Increase £67 by 13%

    b   Decrease $57 by 62%

    c   Decrease 689 kg by 76%

    d   Increase 267 g by 38%

    e   Increase $570 by 8%

    f   Decrease 1780 m by 53%

    g   A TV costs £299 before VAT is added. VAT is 17.5%.
Calculate the cost of the TV after VAT is added.

    h   A holiday costs £3125 but it is reduced by 10% in a sale.
Work out the cost of the holiday when it is in the sale.

2   Evaluate these calculations, giving your answer in standard
form. Do not use a calculator.

    a $(3 \times 10^2) \times (3 \times 10^4)$ **b** $(2.4 \times 10^2) \div (2 \times 10^4)$

    c $(3.2 \times 10^{-4}) \times (3 \times 10^{-2})$ **d** $(9.6 \times 10^{-6}) \div (3.2 \times 10^4)$

3   The table shows the number of words in
each of the first 50 sentences of the novel
The Hobbit by J. R. R. Tolkien.

    a   Calculate an estimate for the mean
number of words per sentence.

    b   Write the modal class.

    c   Write the class interval that
contains the median.

No. of words in sentence	Frequency
1–10	13
11–20	10
21–30	9
31–40	7
41–50	8
51–60	2
61–70	1

4   Write the equation of a line that is parallel to

    a $y = 2x + 5$

    b $y = 4 - 3x$

    c $x + 2y = 1$

5   Divide £480 in these ratios.

    a $2 : 1$ **b** $1 : 5$ **c** $5 : 3$ **d** $7 : 5$

Revision homework

1 Write these ratios in the form $1 : n$.

    a $3 : 9$ **b** $4 : 16$ **c** $5 : 10$ **d** $7 : 21$

    e $10 : 25$ **f** $15 : 60$ **g** $4 : 28$ **h** $6 : 54$

    i $22 : 33$ **j** $18 : 24$ **k** $27 : 45$ **l** $36 : 48$

2 $ABCD$ is a parallelogram.
A is the point $(0, 3)$.
C is the point $(0, -3)$.
The equation of the straight line
through A and B is

$$y = \frac{1}{2}x + 3.$$

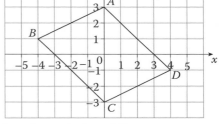

    a   Find the equation of the line
through C and D.

    b   Find the equation of the line passing through A and D.

    c   Calculate the coordinates of the midpoint of the line segment CD.

3 Generate the first five terms of each of these sequences.

    a $T(n) = 4n - 3$ **b** $T(n) = 50 - 3n$ **c** $T(n) = n^2 + 5$

    d $T(n) = (n + 1)(n + 3)$ **e** $T(n) = \dfrac{n}{n+1}$ **f** $T(n) = \dfrac{1}{n^2}$

4   **a**   A shop buys cakes for 50p each and sells them for 89p.
What is the percentage profit?

    b   Paul buys a car for £3995 and sells it one year later for
£3125. Work out the percentage loss.

5 The table shows the
infant mortality rate
(per 100 live births)
and the life
expectancy
in years (at birth)
of 10 countries.

Country	Infant mortality rate	Life expectancy
Australia	4.7	80.4
Denmark	4.6	77.6
Germany	4.2	78.7
Ireland	5.4	77.6
Japan	3.3	81.2
Norway	3.7	79.4
Poland	8.5	74.4
Sweden	2.8	80.4
UK	5.2	78.4
USA	6.5	77.7

    a   Plot this
information
on a scatter graph.

    b   Describe the
relationship between a country's infant mortality
rate and its life expectancy.

8 Revision homework

1 In a primary school class, $\frac{1}{5}$ of the pupils have black hair, $\frac{3}{10}$ of the pupils have blonde hair and $\frac{7}{15}$ of the pupils have brown hair. The rest have red hair.

    a What proportion of the class have red hair?

    b If there are 30 pupils in the class, how many have
       i black hair   **ii** brown hair?

2 Find the missing angles in each of these right-angled triangles, giving your answers to 3 significant figures.

    a   **b**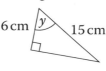

    c    **d**

3 Work out the volume of each cuboid.

    a   **b**   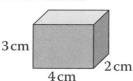   **c**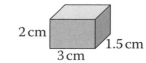

4 Copy and complete each conversion.

    a 45 cm = ___ mm   **b** 2300 cm = ___ m

    c 3500 g = ___ kg   **d** 300 ml = ___ litres

    e 4 tonne = ___ kg   **f** 3.5 km = ___ m

    g 12 000 cm = ___ m   **h** 0.6 litre = ___ ml

5 Write the equations of these lines in order of steepness, starting with the least steep.

    a $y = 4x + 2$ **b** $3x - y = 10$ **c** $y = \frac{1}{2}x + 5$

    d $6y - 2x = 12$ **e** $3y - x = 20$ **f** $y = \frac{3}{4}x - 4$

    g $y - 8x = 5$ **h** $15x - 10y = 20$

Revision homework

1   **a**   Simplify $3a^2b \times 4a^3b^4$

     b   Evaluate

       i $(3^2)^2$ **ii** $(\sqrt{7})^2$

       iii $\sqrt{(2^2 \times 3^2)}$

2   A cylinder of height 15 cm is shown.
The diameter of the circle is 6 cm.
Calculate

     a   the area of the circle

     b   the surface area of the cylinder.

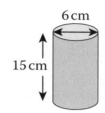

3   Look at these scatter graphs.

   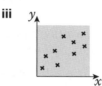

Which scatter graph could represent the relationship
between

     a   height and shoe size

     b   temperature and ice-cream sales

     c   IQ and house number

     d   price and mileage of saloon cars?

4   *ABCD* is a parallelogram.
$AB = CD = 12.4$ cm, $AD = BC = 8.2$ cm. Angle $BAD = 112°$.

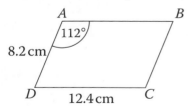

Work out the area of the parallelogram.

> Hint: Find the vertical height using trigonometry.

5   Find the *n*th term for this sequence.
10, 14, 18, 22, 26, 30, ...

1   Given that the equation of a line is $y = 3x + c$, work out the value of c if the line passes through (2, 1).

2   A block of aluminium is in the shape of a cuboid of dimensions 3.4 m by 0.5 m by 2.1 m. Aluminium has a density of 2.7 g/cm³. Work out the mass of the block of aluminium in kilograms.

> Hint: Work out the volume in m³ and then convert to cm³.

3   Finlay sets out at 1 p.m. from Farndon and walks at a speed of 6 km/h to Malpas, 12 km away.
    At 1:30 p.m. Joe jumps on his bike in Malpas and cycles to Farndon, reaching his destination in half an hour.
    a   Construct a distance–time graph to show both journeys.
    b   Work out the average speed at which Joe cycles.
    c   Use your graph to work out when the two boys meet.

4   The diagram shows a solid object.

    a   Sketch the side elevation from the direction marked with an arrow.

    b   Sketch the plan of the solid object.

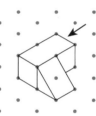

5   Bob has two boxes of whiteboard pens.

    Box number 1 contains 6 pens: 3 red, 2 blue and 1 black.

    Box number 2 contains 12 pens: 5 red, 4 blue and 3 black.

    Bob chooses one pen at random from each box. Calculate the probability that the chosen pens are different colours.

6   A chord AB is drawn inside a circle, centre O, diameter 10 cm.

    The angle $AOB = 47°$.

    Find the length of AB correct to 1 decimal place.

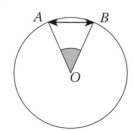